The Architecture of
CASTLES
A Visual Guide

The Architecture of
CASTLES
A Visual Guide

R Allen Brown

B.T. Batsford London

First published 1984

ISBN 0 7134 4089 9

Typeset by Tek-Art Ltd Kent
and printed in Great Britain by
Anchor Brendon Ltd,
Tiptree, Essex
for the publishers
B.T. Batsford Ltd
4 Fitzhardinge Street
London W1H 0AH

Contents

Acknowledgements

The Author and Publishers make grateful acknowledgement to the following for the use of illustrations: Aerofilms Ltd, figs 16, 24, 43, 67, 84, 89, 93, 102; Hallam Ashley, 26, 47; Professor Michél de Bouard of the University of Caen, fig. 5; the British Council, fig. 98; the British Tourist Authority, fig. 35; Caisse Nationale des Monuments Historique, fig. 19; committee for Aerial Photography, University of Cambridge, figs 1, 2, 8, 11, 17, 77, 103; J. Allen Cash Ltd, fig. 53; Department of the Environment, 3, 9, 10, 13, 20, 21, 22, 27, 31, 38, 54, 73; T. Edmondson, fig. 65; Exeter City Council, fig. 56; Fox Photos Ltd, fig. 11; Leonard and Marjorie Gayton, figs 36, 45, 68, 72, 80, 92, 99; A.F. Kersting, FRPS, figs 25, 28, 39, 41, 62, 66, 94, 101; Mustograph Agency, figs 44, 100; Roger Schall, fig. 75; Trustees of the British Museum, figs 105, 106. Figs 29, 30, 40, 42, 51, 52, 55, 63, 76, 78, 79, 81, 83, 85, 87, 90 are Crown Copyright, reproduced by permission of the Controller of Her Majesty's Stationery Office.

1 The Castle in History

Although this book is intended as a kind of architectural handbook which he who runs may read – and others even in motor-cars may glance at – there is in fact little or no point in looking at buildings divorced from their proper history. All buildings reflect the society which produced them, and none can be understood without some knowledge of that society. The effort required is richly rewarding, moreover, for architecture is itself a part of history, direct evidence of, and immediate access to the past. The contemplation of historic buildings thus sets up a two-way process in the mind of the beholder: the more one knows about the society which created them, the better they will be understood; and the more informed one's contemplation and inspection of them, the deeper and more appreciative will become one's knowledge of the period from which they derive.

The need to make the effort is particularly true of castles, for they are probably at once the best known and least understood of medieval monuments. Everyone has some notion of the purpose and function of a church or a great house even if his actual knowledge of, let us say, the liturgy and theology of medieval catholicism, or the lifestyle of an eighteenth-century aristocrat, is sadly scanty. With castles it is otherwise, and even worse, and they suffer especially from that near-universal ignorance of the so-called 'Middle Ages' which is characteristic of our philistine age and concomitant educational system. Nowadays, to call anything 'medieval' is itself an insult, while to call it 'feudal' is ten times more offensive; and if castles are not seen merely as vaguely romantic ruins, they are seen through an idiot haze of bold, bad barons, deep and dismal dungeons, and boiling oil. At best their context is thought to be almost exclusively military, and that too is against them, since in our time one must be against warfare as one used to be against sin.

Let us therefore devote a few pages to a brief pursuit and capture of the truth. The first thing to say and insist is that the castle was always a residence as well as a fortress, that its residential role was at least as fundamental as the military and at least 50 per cent of its purpose. The castle, in short, if we wish to define it (and we must), was a fortified residence and a residential fortress and this duality is essential to it and to our understanding of it. The fact that a great man, for whatever reason, wished to live or spend part of his time there, may, for a start, go a long way to explain why any given castle is where it is, as well as more obviously explaining the abundance of grand residential accommodation that will invariably be found within it, or the fact that the fortunate few still do live in castles. Words as well as buildings comprise history, and in France and the French language the word *château* has come to mean any large house of a certain pretension. In the long, complex process of the decline of the castle in the so-called late 'medieval' and early 'modern' periods, what actually happened

1 *An aerial view (1948) of Pevensey, Sussex, from the west. The castle was planted in 1066 within the much larger enclosure of the former Roman camp of Anderida, then an Anglo-Saxon burgh (cf. Portchester). The present walls and towers are thirteenth century and the ruined keep (top) twelfth.*

or city, but one man, albeit a great man, his family, his guests, his household and retainers. It is, as we shall see, above all a centre of lordship, but meanwhile it is its private as opposed to communal nature, and its residential function, which set it apart from all other known types of fortification in the history of the West, both earlier and later. To dismiss the latter first, all modern fortifications – in England, let us say from the Tudor coastal forts of the sixteenth century onwards (fig. 93) – are purely military fortresses and have no residential function in the domestic sense. Similarly in earlier periods Roman fortifications are public military works with no domestic residential function, and their walled cities, towns and camps obviously communal fortifications, as are Iron Age fortresses, Anglo-Saxon burghs, Henry the Fowler's derivative fortresses in Germany, and Viking camps. Often the difference is still visible to the naked eye since the difference between private and communal must often be one of scale, as when, for example, in England the Normans planted their relatively small castles within the pre-existing and far larger Roman and Anglo-Saxon fortifications of Pevensey (fig. 1) or Portchester (fig. 2) or London, or within the Iron Age ramparts of Dover (fig. 77) or Old Sarum (fig. 3).

The domestically residential role of the castle is fundamental to it, and equally fundamental – but not more – is its military. That military purpose is well known but seldom fully understood. While everybody knows about the castle's defensive function in resisting a siege (fig. 106), that is only half at most, and probably less then half, of its military role. It is true that considerations of defensive strength determine the castle's plan, form and architectural development, for it is a stronghold which must successfully resist attack as necessary; but the fundamental military purpose of that stronghold is offensive rather than defensive, to control the surrounding countryside by means of the mounted men within it. This explains the high proportion in garrisons of knights and other mounted men-at-arms who obviously do not need their horses to defend the castle's walls and towers (though they may make sorties and forays since the

was that the military importance of the castle faded away, to leave it either increasingly ruined and abandoned or as a stately home, obsolete but with a particular claim to ancient nobility. The castle in the days of its dominance was the fortified residence of a lord – any lord, by no means necessarily the king or prince – and we must add that it was seriously fortified, able to withstand armies, for there were always those half-way houses lightly or moderately defended for the sake of domestic security but not regarded by contemporaries as proper castles. We as historians call such places 'fortified manors' (figs 98, 99), and their spirit is that of Patrick Forbes before rebuilding the plundered Corse Castle in Aberdeenshire in *c.* 1500: 'Please God, I will build me such a house as thieves will need to knock at ere they enter.'

As the fortified residence of a lord, the castle had what we can only call a private as opposed to a communal function: it sheltered not a community of many families like a town

best defence is not always passive), and the range of the castle in this respect is the range of the war-horse carrying an armoured rider – say ten miles if you wish to return before nightfall and more if you do not. Warfare was and is about the control of the land, and in the feudal period he who would control the land must first hold, or take, the castles. Hence all those sieges, and the castle dominates the warfare of the age because it dominates the land. One may thus begin to see the supreme military (and therefore political) value of the castle, achieved, moreover, with an important economy of manpower. Because of the developing strength of fortification, because throughout the period of the castle's ascendancy defence was in the ascendant over attack, garrisons could be and were comparatively small; yet that small force could and did hold the district in which it was based unless it was locked up by a full-scale and prolonged investment involving a far greater force, which it was difficult to bring to bear and still more difficult to sustain. In the event, it took King John, who was no mean soldier especially in the art of siege-craft, almost two months in October and November 1215 to take Rochester castle, vitally placed to command the crossing of the Medway and

the south-eastern approaches to London. In the siege of Kenilworth in 1266 – a last-ditch affair of honour and despair on the part of the defenders – the castle held out for no less than six months, and then only yielded upon terms, against all the force of his father's kingdom which the young Lord Edward, son of Henry III, could muster.

In its military role as in its residential role, and still more in the combination and total integration of the two, the castle demonstrates its feudality. The warfare of the feudal period in the West, from the tenth and eleventh centuries, let us say, to the fifteenth, was dominated by heavy cavalry and castles. The élite of the former, especially in the earlier centuries, were the knights (fig. 4), superbly mounted and equipped, with the full-time training and dedicated horsemanship (both from youth up) necessary to fight effectively on

3   *An aerial photograph of Old Sarum (i.e. the original Salisbury) in Wiltshire shows the comparatively small enclosure of the Norman castle within the much larger enclosure of the pre-Conquest burgh. Also within the latter the foundations of the Norman cathedral can be clearly seen.*

4   *Norman knights before Hastings in 1066, from the Bayeux Tapestry. A military and therefore a social élite, the knights are shown mounted on splendid war-horses and each expensively equipped with mail hauberk, conical helmet, long shield, lance (and sword). Note the built-up saddles, and long stirrups to give a secure seat especially in the shock combat of the charge.*

horseback, and whose specialist shock-tactic of the charge with couched lance (locked under the arm, all momentum of heavy horse and rider focused at the point) was expected to carry all before it in the field and usually did. Feudalism in the beginning was all about knights, the provision and maintenance of this highly expensive military commodity. Knights and castles go together, as we have seen, and doubly so: for while castles were the fortified bases from which the mobility of knights might operate, yet also they were in themselves an answer to cavalry which otherwise dominated warfare. Anna Comnena, daughter of the Eastern Emperor at Constantinople, in the early twelfth century, much impressed by what she had seen and heard, declared in striking phrase that the charging Frankish knight would pierce the walls of Babylon; but in reality one could not take a castle by a cavalry charge. Further this military élite, riding proudly in the full panoply of war, were a social élite also, exclusive because expensive. The knights constituted the secular ruling-class of feudal Europe, for if not all knights were great men, all great men were knights. And great men – kings and princes, earls and counts and barons, with other knights in their train – were the lords of castles. The castle is surely the appropriate setting for this military aristocracy whose members were

5   *Doué-la-Fontaine (Maine-et-Loire) is the oldest known castle. Stone-built from the beginning, the building shown was originally a ground-floor hall type of lordly residence, but was fortified in c. 950 by heightening into a strong tower with the residential apartments at first-floor level (now gone again), like Langeais (fig. 6).*

required to be both lords and mounted warriors, and never shows its feudality more than in that combination of noble residence and fortress which is unique to it.

The feudality of the castle may also be demonstrated by date; that is to say, the period of its dominance in peace and war coincides with that period in the history of the West which for other reasons we call feudal. The earliest surviving castles in Europe, at Doué-la-Fontaine (fig. 5) and Langeais (fig. 6), both in France and in the area of the Loire valley, date from the second half of the tenth century, the time of the establishment of feudal society and of the formation of those new feudal principalities into which France was to be divided (in this case the counties of Blois and Anjou respectively), created by the imposition of new lordship by means of knights and castles and the bonds of vassalage. At Doué-la-Fontaine, indeed, we may see from the recent spectacular excavations the origin of the castle before our eyes, as a previously unfortified late-Carolingian lordly residence, burnt out in war, was fortified and

6 *Langeais (Indre-et-Loire), attributed to Fulk 'the Black', Count of Anjou, in c. 1000, is the second-oldest known castle (cf. Doué-la-Fontaine). What remains standing of that date is the stone-built keep, shown here, in form a strong hall with the residential apartments at first-floor level.*

made into a strong tower about the year 950 by Theobald, count of Blois. At the other end of the spectrum the decline of the castle coincides with the decline of feudal society itself – in England, let us say, in the sixteenth and seventeenth centuries – and is to be attributed to that, and not to the introduction of gunpowder three centuries before.

The residences of kings, princes and magnates, the centres at need of their military power, the centres also of social life and of much local government, of rents and services and the nexus of feudal obligations – there is no doubt that castles stood for lordship in men's minds and were the expression as well as much of the substance of lordly power and control. 'You shall have the lordship in castle and in tower,' said the envoys of Henry II's rebellious son, seeking to win over the King of Scots to their enterprise by the offer of the northern counties of England. The contemporary word applied to the architecturally dominant feature of a castle – often, but not always, a great tower – is *donjon*; the word still survives

more or less unsullied in France (cf. the baseless connotations of close confinement and durance vile now attached to the English 'dungeon') and is derived from the Latin *dominium*, meaning lordship. Castles tend to be ignored by medieval architectural historians, presumably on the ground that as purely functional buildings they have nothing to do with art. Setting aside the facts that churches are functional also, and that castles contained individual buildings, including chapels, as fine as the age could make them (e.g. St George's Chapel, Windsor, fig. 88) we may urge that medieval military architecture is as deliberately symbolic as ecclesiastical, and for that and other reasons deserves to be taken as seriously.

2 The Origins of the Castle

FRANCE

The castle, then, is the fortified residence of a lord and a manifestation of feudal society and more especially feudal lordship. For its origins in Western Europe where it belongs we go back at least to the mid-tenth century and perhaps earlier. It was in 864, in the Capitulary (ordinance or decree) of Pistes, that Charles the Bald, King of the West Franks, prohibited the construction of fortifications without his permission and ordered their destruction: 'We will and expressly command that whoever at this time has made castles (*castella*) and fortifications (*firmitates*) and enclosures (*haias*) without our permission shall have them demolished by the First of August.' There can be no certainty, however, that this is the first written reference to castles proper, for there is the problem of words, vocabulary and nomenclature, which may be slow to adapt to changes in fact, history and society. At anytime between the ninth century and at least the eleventh, ancient and classical Latin words like *castrum, castellum, municipium, munitio* and *oppidum* could of course continue to be used for any kind of fortress, strongplace or town, as well as possibly for the new castle. What the Edict of Pistes does seem to indicate, however, is the advent of private and unauthorized fortification, raised by other than royal and public authority, and thereby hangs a tale. In the Roman world, as in the modern, fortification and military power were held to be a monopoly of the state, and this attitude was maintained by the Germanic successor states of Rome in the West which culminate in the great empire of Charlemagne or Charles the Great (crowned Emperor on Christmas Day 800 at Rome). Soon after his death, however, Charlemagne's empire broke up, and at the Treaty of Verdun in 853 a tripartite division was recognized as the kingdom of the West Franks (which will be France), the kingdom of the East Franks (which will be Germany), and the Middle Kingdom extending from the Low Countries to Italy inclusive. In Charles the Bald's kingdom of the West Franks fragmentation was to continue, not least as the result of devastating external assaults by Vikings, by Magyars and by Muslims. The concept of kingship, hallowed by the Church, remained, but political reality was increasingly by the tenth century not the kingdom but the feudal principalities into which it became divided: Normandy, Blois, Chartres, Champagne, Anjou, Poitou, Brittany and the rest. As the effective power of the kings declined, society became more and more based upon local territorial lordship, and the new princes, in carving out their new principalities, assuredly took over the regalian rights of military service and fortification along with others, and reinforced them with the potent powers of feudalism.

In the brave new world of feudal society now becoming established in West Frankia and in northern France especially (thence to spread south and east, and ultimately north and west) the ancient concept of king or prince and subject was never allowed to die, but political and social reality became increasingly a personal and local lordship binding man to man. From one point of view feudalism can be seen as the institutionalization of personal loyalty and obligation, and society, at the top where it mattered most, was held together and disciplined above all by the bonds binding vassals to lords in the feudal hierarchy. Up and down the scale vassals were bound to their lords by the solemn ceremony of commendation, comprising the act of homage (to become the man of another) confirmed by the oath of fealty, and to which investiture with the fief might be added. They received maintenance, which is support, protection and livelihood, and, if they were lucky, land, which is the fief, to be held of the lord as his tenant. They owed in return many services, including aid, counsel, escort and, pre-eminently, military service which was increasingly knight-service. That knight-service might be rendered either in the field or in the castle. The princes of the developing feudal principalities derived huge powers, and those not only military, from their position at the top of the hierarchy as feudal suzerains, the lords of lords, and by these means more than by lingering notions of regality and ancient titles like count, their new principalities were formed and held together. Vassalage and knights – and castles – were the means of the new order. And certainly castles, by the mid-tenth century, were becoming a familiar feature of the landscape at least in northern France as the centres of new lordship, riveting one's rule upon the land which they controlled by the knights based upon them.

The process can be seen at work, as an instance, in the formation of the county of Anjou in the course of the tenth century, and especially in the career of one of its greatest early counts and co-founder, Fulk Nerra, 'the Black' (987-1040), who has been called a 'pioneer in the art of feudal government' (R.W. Southern, *The Making of the Middle Ages*, London, 1953, p. 86). His grandson later wrote of him that he built thirteen castles, which were then listed, as well as others too numerous to name. Those listed are Langeais (fig. 6), Baugé, Château-

Gontier, Chaumont, Durtal, Faye, Maulévrier, Mirebeau, Moncontour, Montrésor, Montreuil-Bellay, Passavant and Sainte-Maure. The many others are nowadays thought to have included La-Motte-Montboyau, Montbazon (fig. 19), Montrichard, Mateflon, Saint-Florent-le-Vieux and Trèves. Here, then, is the context of one of the earliest surviving castles in Europe, at Langeais in the county of Anjou, and a similar context pertains to the earliest of all, at Doué-la-Fontaine (figs. 5 and 6). Fulk Nerra's neighbours were similarly fortifying key points of their domains, and it is Anjou's enemy, the count of Blois, who is thought to have first fortified Doué-la-Fontaine as a castle – eventually to be taken, it is also thought, by Fulk Nerra in *c.*1025.

The process of encastellation as part and parcel of the formation of feudal states and the establishment of feudal society can also be seen in Normandy, which is particularly our concern if we seek the origin of castles in England. The history of the future duchy of Normandy itself begins at the traditional date of 911, with the grant of territory for settlement by the West Frankish king, Charles the Simple, to the Viking raiders of the Seine valley under their leader, Rollo. In the following century these Norsemen were to make of their territory the most potent feudal principality in France, chiefly by the adoption and adaptation of Frankish religion, Frankish laws, Frankish feudalism and Frankish warfare, in the process themselves becoming Normans, and more Frankish than the Franks. As part of this development, the growing power of the Norman count or duke is marked by, amongst other things, the castles which he raised. The principal ducal palace at Fécamp was evidently fortified in the tenth century, probably by Duke Richard I 'the Fearless' (942-96) who built the great tower at Rouen, and there is reference also (at a time when written sources are rare) to a third fortified palace, i.e. castle, built by the same prince at Bayeux. It was in Richard I's time also that the castle of Ivry was first raised and conferred upon his half-brother Raoul d'Ivry. Under Dukes Richard II (996-1026) and Richard III (1026-7) the castles of Tillières, Falaise, Le Homme (now l'Isle

Marie), Cherbourg and Brix were founded. Robert I 'the Magnificent' (1027-35) added Cherrueix at least, while in famous legend it was at the castle of Falaise that he first formed his liason with Arlette so that in consequence, and most appropriately, it was there that the future Conqueror was born (though visitors to Falaise should note that the happy event most certainly did not take place in the present keep built almost a century later). As for Duke William the Conqueror himself, we may cite, as one more example of the association of castles and lordship, his fortification soon after 1047 of the town of Caen and his planting there of a great castle – a veritable fortified palace again – as the principal centre of ducal authority henceforth to be asserted over Lower Normandy.

It is nowadays maintained, especially by French historians, that castles like other good things in life begin at the top of society, i.e. with kings and princes, and only later spread downwards to other and lesser magnates. Whether or not this is true (and it may not be a universal truth, being altogether too schematically tidy), it is certain that in Normandy by the mid-eleventh century castles were held by other lords than the duke. As a general instance, a recent study of the district of the Cinglais, in Lower Normandy between Caen and Falaise, has shown the foundation of some 26 castles there in the course of the eleventh century, mostly in the first half. They represent the taking-in and cultivation of new land, and stand as the centres of the comparatively minor new lordships by which this was done. As a particular instance, there is the castle of Le Plessis-Grimoult in the same area; it has also been the object of recent study and archaeological excavation. It is securely dated to before 1047 because in that year it is known to have been abandoned, having been confiscated from its lord, Grimoult du Plessis, for his unsuccessful rebellion against the young Duke William. Again it was the centre, or, in the language of feudalism, *caput* (head), of a new lordship or 'honour', held not direct of the duke but of the bishop of Bayeux, and again the lordship consisted chiefly of newly colonized land on the margins of ancient settlement.

Such instances further emphasize the residential and social role of the castle as an integral part of the new order and the new lordship. But feudal lords were also by definition warriors, and the military role of the castle is well enough brought out by other evidence of their increasing presence in Normandy in the earlier eleventh century. Writing of the civil wars which racked the duchy in the disputed succession which followed the untimely death (1035) of Robert the Magnificent, and thus during the minority of his designated heir, William the Conqueror, the contemporary Norman historians tell us of the many castles which were then illegedly raised. 'In his early youth', says William of Jumièges of young Duke William, 'many of the Normans, renouncing their fealty to him, raised earthworks (*aggeres*) in many places and constructed the safest castles (*munitiones*).' The same historian (to be echoed by another, William of Poitiers) celebrates the victory of Val-ès-Dunes in 1047, whereby the duke won his supremacy, with the remark, 'a happy battle indeed which in a single day brought about the collapse of so many castles.' For the castles raised against him and without his licence during the wars were afterwards demolished (like Le Plessis-Grimoult). In the feudal state the ancient and pre-feudal principle that fortification is the prerogative of the prince was neither forgotten nor allowed to lapse, and we know from later but retrospective evidence that in Normandy under the rule of William the Conqueror castles could not be raised without the duke's permission, and those which were thus licensed must be made over to him on demand. 'No-one might raise a castle (*castellum*) in Normandy', roundly declares the 'Laws and Customs' drawn up in 1091 as a statement of ducal rights in the duchy in the Conqueror's day, 'and no-one in Normandy might withhold the possession of his castle from the lord of Normandy if he wished to take it into his hand'.

ENGLAND

In England – and subsequently the rest of Britain – there is really no doubt that castles were introduced by the Normans, along with feudalism, as one of the results of the

Norman Conquest. Old English society on the eve of 1066, reinforced by the Viking invasions and settlements of the ninth and early eleventh centuries, was still pre-feudal and its monarchy still Carolingian in type and, indeed, in power. While kingship had waned in West Frankia under the hammer-blows of Viking, Magyar and Muslim incursions and its own internal divisions, English kingship had gone from strength to strength as Alfred of Wessex and his successors had conquered the 'Danelaw' (the area of Viking settlement) and imposed their rule over all England. Institutionally the conquest by Cnut in 1016, fifty years before the Norman Conquest, had made no difference to the notion of a united kingdom, potent by the standards of the age, and in 1042 Edward 'the Confessor' had returned (from his exile in Normandy) to the throne of his fathers. There was thus no occasion in England for that reformation of society and political power from the bottom upwards on the basis of local and feudal military lordship which had taken place across the Channel. In England, thus, all military service was the king's, and so was all fortification, both of them part of a national system of royal rights and common obligations. That military service, moreover, was infantry service of the ancient kind, for there had been in England no revolutionary change in military tactics, no adoption of the new Frankish techniques of mounted warfare, of heavy cavalry and knights, with all the attendant social consequences. Fortification, too, was not only a royal monopoly but was equally of the ancient and traditional kind – communal fortifications, known as burghs, and in effect fortified towns.

The origin of the castle in England is the Norman Conquest, and the only known and certain castles before 1066 are that best type of exception which proves the rule, i.e. castles founded by Norman and French lords already in England, the so-called favourites of Edward the Confessor, the *avant garde* of the Conquest and the pioneers of Norman penetration. There were very few such castles and they comprised a group in Herefordshire consisting of Hereford itself, Ewyas Harold, Richard's Castle and at least one other, i.e. the castles which Ralph 'the

Timid', (King Edward's nephew made earl of Hereford), and his companions built on the borders of south Wales; together probably with Clavering in Essex, the castle of Robert fitz Wimarc. The native source of the Anglo-Saxon Chronicle mentions these castles in resentful terms as new, foreign and oppressive ('the foreigners then had built a castle in Herefordshire in earl Swein's province and had inflicted every possible injury and insult upon the king's men in those parts'), while later the well-informed Ordericus Vitalis was to attribute the very success of the Norman Conquest at least partly to the lack of castles in England: 'the fortresses which the Gauls call castles had been very few in the English provinces, and for this reason the English, although warlike and courageous, had nevertheless shown themselves too weak to withstand their enemies.'

Further, the positive evidence for the introduction of castles into England by the Normans in and after 1066 is simply overwhelming. Amongst the first acts of the Normans after their disembarkation at Pevensey (fig. 1) on 28 September 1066, was the raising of a castle within the Old English burgh and former Roman fortress, and when a few days later they moved their camp to Hastings they raised another there (again within an existing Old English burgh), as shown dramatically on the Bayeux Tapestry (fig. 7). Immediately after his great victory at Hastings the Conqueror marched to occupy Dover and there planted another castle in the burgh on the cliff-top (fig. 77), and before his triumphal entry into London for his coronation (which took place on Christmas Day, 1066, at Westminster) he sent an advance party ahead to raise a castle in the city. In this last we may see the origin of the royal castle of London – later the Tower of London (fig. 74) – and soon there were to be two other castles there, Baynard's Castle in the south-west corner and Montfichet to the north of it. From then on as from the beginning every stage of the Norman Conquest and subsequent settlement is marked by the castles which were raised, north, south, east, west, and on into Wales, for castles (and the knights within them) were the very means whereby new Norman

and French lordship was imposed upon the potentially hostile countryside. Ordericus Vitalis describes how the Norman king 'rode to all the remote parts of the kingdom and fortified suitable places against enemy attacks', and William of Poitiers says how 'in [his] castles he placed capable custodians, brought over from France, in whose loyalty no less than ability he trusted, together with large numbers of horse and foot.' Domesday Book (1087), the Conqueror's majestic survey of his new kingdom and its resources, records over and over again the number of houses and tenements destroyed in towns and cities to make way for the new castles placed in them (166 at Lincoln, 113 at Norwich), and as early as 1074 we are given an authentic glimpse of the network of castles covering the country in the Anglo-Saxon Chronicle's account of the journey of

7 *The raising of Hastings' castle in 1066 from the Bayeux Tapestry. The castle is represented by its motte which already bears a timber palisade about its summit. The method of construction of the motte in a series of rammed-down layers is to be noted.*

the English Prince Edgar and his household from Scotland to Normandy: 'and the sheriff of York came to meet them at Durham and went all the way with them and had them provided with food and fodder at every castle they came to until they got overseas to the king.'

For the native English no less than for the Norman *conquistadores* the new castles were the symbols as well as the substance of new lordship, and the Anglo-Saxon Chronicle, which, after 1066, comes to provide a kind of worm's eye-view of the Conquest, laments the oppressive hegemony they represent. They 'built castles far and wide throughout the country', reads an entry for 1067 'and

8 *Pleshey, Essex, from the west (1961). The splendid but typical motte-and-bailey site stands up clearly on the left, with the formerly fortified township to the right. The whole provides a dramatic example of the impact of Norman lordship on the English countryside.*

the total. In terms of organization, labour and resources alone the raising of hundreds of castles across the length and breadth of the land at more or less the same time is impressive. It must represent, indeed, the greatest and most concentrated castle-building programme in the whole history of the West, for, by contrast, in France the progress of feudalism and encastellation was a natural and long-term growth, while the Norman conquest of southern Italy and Sicily was a much more piecemeal and less systematic process than their conquest of England, and was spread over almost a century. It is inconceivable that castle-building on this scale – three in London, two in York – would have been carried out if castles had already been a feature of Old English and Anglo-Scandinavian society before the Normans came. And if for the native English the new castles rising on every side were the signs and symbols of a new and alien rule, so for the historian they are the signs and symbols of the Norman Conquest

9 *The Conqueror's White Tower (which gives its name to 'The Tower of London') from the south-east, with the remains of the Wardrobe Tower in the foreground. The external timber stairway has recently been constructed to suggest the original entrance arrangement at first-floor level.*

distressed the wretched folk, and always after that it grew much worse. May the end be good when God wills!' The same note is struck by the same Chronicle in its obituary of William the Conqueror:

> He had castles built
> And poor men hard oppressed

– and we may still hear echoing faintly across the ages the curse of the English Archbishop Ealdred of York, recorded by William of Malmesbury and laid upon Urse d'Abbetot, for raising the castle at Worcester so close to the cathedral church that it encroached upon the monks' cemetery: 'Hattest thou Urs, have thou God's kurs.' In truth the number of castles raised in England and the marches of Wales in the decades after 1066 as part and parcel of the Conquest was prodigious. Entirely casual and unsystematic references to castles in the Domesday Book amount to 50, and similarly casual references in all the extant written sources by the end of the century amount to some 84, yet it is known that these figures are only mere fractions of and stand for all it stands for – the introduction and imposition not merely of Norman rule but of a new ruling class, a new military and political system, new lordship and thereby a new type of society which we call feudal. And like the Norman Conquest itself they have lasted. Some, like Windsor (fig. 88) or Arundel (fig. 102) or Alnwick, are still proudly upstanding and occupied by the descendants or successors of the princes and lords who founded them; but there is not a county which cannot show at least the remains or traces of early castles dating from the first century of English feudalism and often the first strenuous days after 1066. If one wants a visible, vivid impression of the impact of the Norman Conquest upon the English countryside and Old English society, one cannot do better than contemplate some of them, like Pleshey in Essex (fig. 8), for example, where literally everything is new after Hastings – castle, fortified township and even the French name – set down in a place which did not exist until the first Mandeville lord chose it as the centre or *caput* of his new territorial lordship. So too the majesty of the Conqueror and the ethos of the Norman Conquest is nowhere better felt than in the White Tower (fig. 9), *the* Tower of London, which he built and in whose Chapel of St John the Evangelist (fig. 10) he must have often prayed to the Norman God of Battles.

10　*The Chapel of St John in the White Tower at second-floor level and little altered since the Conqueror's day.*

3 Early Castles

It is often assumed that all early castles were of earthwork and timber construction only, as opposed to masonry, and, further, that they conformed to the type known as the 'motte-and-bailey' (fig. 11). In fact the assumption is wrong on both counts. The two earliest surviving castles in Europe, at Doué-la-Fontaine and Langeais (dating from the second half of the tenth century, figs. 5 and 6), both have as we shall see contemporary stone buildings, which, moreover, take the form of strong towers. Fortification in stone was thus evidently there from the beginning. Further, not all early castles constructed of earthworks with timber buildings and defences have mottes, i.e. great earthen mounds, as their dominant feature and strongpoint, and thus do not belong to the ubiquitous motte-and-bailey type. It is, in any case, a mistake to distinguish sharply between 'earthwork-and-timber castles' and 'stone castles', and certainly mistaken to see the fundamental development of castles in the earlier centuries of their existence, between, say, the tenth and twelfth centuries inclusive, as being universally one from earthwork and timber to stone. Not only was stone fortification and building present from the beginning in some instances, but also timber works could be undertaken very late, as was the case with Edward I's 'peel' at Linlithgow in Scotland, built in 1302. Further yet, the two modes of construction might be combined in any period, and indeed there are few, if any, castles, even at the apogee of medieval military architecture in stone, which do not employ earthworks also, in the form of moats, ditches and banks. And certainly neither the role of the castle nor the principles of its fortification alter with, nor depend upon, the materials used in its construction.

MOTTE-AND-BAILEY CASTLES

Nevertheless, there is abundant evidence to show that both in France and, later, in England and Wales, castles of earthwork and timber predominated in the beginning, and that, in England and Wales especially, the great majority of early castles followed the motte-and-bailey plan (741 with mottes as opposed to 205 without are the latest figures from field studies of castles raised between 1066 and 1215). We will therefore start with that, as the best-known type of early castle and as the most easily recognizable of mere archaeological castle sites, where all standing buildings and defences have gone.

The dominant feature is, of course, the motte, a great (sometimes not so great) mound of earth or rock, wholly artificial or partly natural, with a deep ditch (wet or dry) about its base as a further defence. In the first generation at least its superstructure, the buildings and defences upon its summit, are likely to have been of timber, and in that case never survive. Nevertheless, contemporary illustrations, not least on the Bayeux Tapestry (fig. 12), contemporary literary descriptions, and modern archaeological excavations, enable us to have some

11 *A model example of a motte-and-bailey site at Hallaton (Castle Hill) in Leicestershire.*

knowledge of them, even if we are not able accurately to reconstruct them. A strong timber palisade, with wall walks and perhaps projecting towers, crowned the motte, and within this, standing more or less centrally, there would be a great timber tower. Thus Walter the archdeacon, in his Life of John, bishop of Thérouanne, written about 1130, tells us that his master was often accustomed to stay at 'Merchem' (Merekem near Dixmude or Merckerghem near Dunkirk?) and that:

There was, near the porch of the church, a fortress which we may call a castle . . . exceedingly high, built after the custom of that land by the lord of the town many years before. For it is the habit of the magnates and nobles of those parts . . . to raise a mound of earth as high as they can and surround it with a ditch as broad and deep as possible. The top of this mound they completely enclose with a palisade of hewn logs bound close together like a wall, with towers set in its

circuit so far as the site permits. In the middle of the space within the palisade they build a residence, or, dominating everything, keep.

That the tower upon the motte, usually if not always the residence of the lord of the castle himself, could be an elaborate and imposing edifice, albeit of timber, is shown by the late-eleventh-century illustrations on the Bayeux Tapestry – not least in its depiction of the castle of Bayeux (fig. 12) – by fragments of a mid-twelfth-century *dolce vita* revealed by modern excavations at South Mimms in Middlesex, and by a number of contemporary descriptions. The timber tower-house of the castle of La Cour-Marigny, near Montargis, in the mid-eleventh century, we are told, was of two storeys, the ground floor containing a storeroom and the upper floor the 'solar' where the noble lord of the castle lived, conversing, eating and sleeping with his household. Laurence, prior of Durham, wrote of the timber tower on the motte of the castle there, that 'each face is girded by a beautiful gallery which is fixed in the warlike

12 William, duke of Normandy, the feudal prince, superbly armed and mounted as a knight, enters his city of Bayeux in 1064. The city is represented by its castle and the castle by its motte – with an elaborate towered superstructure upon it. (From the Bayeux Tapestry.)

wall'. Most elaborate of all, however, is the contemporary description by Lambert of Ardres of the 'great and lofty house' which Arnold, lord of Ardres, built on the motte of his castle of Ardres about the year 1117:

Later, when peace had been established between Manasses Count of Guisnes and Arnold lord of Ardres, Arnold built upon the motte at Ardres a timber house which was a marvellous example of the carpenter's craft and excelled in materials used all contemporary houses in Flanders. It was designed and built by a carpenter from Bourbourg called Louis, who fell little short of Daedalus in his skill; for he created an almost impenetrable labyrinth, piling storeroom upon storeroom, chamber upon chamber, room upon room, extending the larders and granaries into cellars and building the chapel in a convenient place overlooking all else from high up on the eastern side. He made it of three floors, the topmost storey supported by the second as though suspended in the air. The first storey was at ground level, and here were the cellars and granaries, the great chests, casks, butts and other domestic utensils. On the second floor were the residential apartments and common living quarters, and there were the larders, the rooms of the bakers and the butlers, and the great chamber of the lord and his lady, where they slept, on to which adjoined a small room which provided the sleeping quarters of the maidservants and children. Here in the inner part of the great chamber there was a small private room where at early dawn or in the evening, or in sickness, or for warming the maids and weaned children, they used to light a fire. On this floor also was the kitchen, which was on two levels. On the lower level pigs were fattened, geese tended, chickens and other fowls killed or prepared. On the upper levels the cooks and stewards worked and prepared the delicate dishes for the lords, which entailed much hard work on the part of the cooks, and here also the meals for the household and servants were prepared each day. On the top floor of the house there were small rooms in which, on one side, the sons of the lord slept when they wished to do so, and, on the other side, his daughters as they were obliged. There too the watchman, the servants appointed to keep the household, and the ever-ready guards, took their sleep when they could. There were stairs and corridors from floor to floor, from the residential quarters to the kitchen, from chamber to chamber, and from the main building to the *loggia*, where they used to sit for conversation and recreation (and which is well named, for the word is derived from *logos* meaning speech), as also from the *loggia* to the oratory or chapel, which was like the temple of Solomon in its ceiling and its decoration.

At Ardres in the early twelfth century the whole self-sufficient household of a lord and his immediate family is apparently housed in the great timber tower on the motte, yet however skilled Louis the carpenter from Bourbourg may have been – or the master masons who designed and built the similar great towers of stone which we examine later – not all the lavish needs of feudal lordship could be confined within a tower, however grand and ingeniously contrived. Room has to be found for the expanded military contingent of the household in time of war, for guests with their own attendant households, for the resident staff, including the constable, who will be in charge in the frequent absences of the lord, and, not least, for the horses of all these people. The motte and its superstructure, which usually includes the lord's privy residence as at Ardres, is deliberately the dominant feature and strongpoint of the whole castle which will necessarily comprise also one or more baileys or main enclosures. The motte is connected to the bailey by a bridge or causeway crossing the ditch (shown clearly on the Bayeux Tapestry), and the enclosure of the bailey is heavily defended by its own ditch and bank, with a palisade crowning the latter and strengthened by wall-walk and towers. Within, there will stand all those other extensive buildings required, again of timber construction in the classic motte-and-bailey castle as conceived by archaeologists and historians – great hall and church or chapel for general assembly, chamber blocks, kitchen, storehouses and stables. A multiplicity of residential accommodation is *de rigeur* in castles and a necessity of the way of life of the lords who occupied them, continually on the move with

their households, their *mesnil*, from one place to the next.

In the classic model of the motte-and-bailey castle, as at Pleshey in Essex (fig. 8) and a hundred other places, the motte is artificial (constructed, it may be, of a series of rammed-down layers of earth, as it is at Pleshey, and as it is shown under construction at Hastings on the Bayeux Tapestry, fig. 7), roughly circular and roughly like a flat-topped cone or upturned pudding-basin in shape. It rises, free standing, with its own ditch about its base, adjacent and to one side of the larger enclosure of the bailey, which is bean- or kidney-shaped. The whole is thus not unlike a figure of eight in plan (fig. 11), but there are variations, not only in the shape but also in the number and disposition of the elements. At Bramber (the centre, head or *caput* of one of the Sussex 'rapes' or compact lordships, put into the hands of William de Braose by the Conqueror after the Conquest) the motte stands wholly within the bailey, as it does at Aldingbourne, also in Sussex, though this is unusual. At royal Windsor and at Arundel (*caput* of the Sussex rape of Roger of Montgomery after 1066, fig. 102) there are two baileys, one on either side of the motte, and this is evidently not a sign of particular grandeur because the same arrangement occurs at the comparatively minor castle of Grimbosc in Normandy (in the Cinglais area), which also dates from the mid-eleventh century. A double ditch about both motte and bailey as at Berkhamsted (fig. 13) and Hen Domen (the latter the mid-eleventh-century precursor of Montgomery castle, fig. 14) is a rare feature, and so is the distinction of two mottes, found at Lincoln and at Lewes (the last again the centre of a Sussex rape, this time given by the Conqueror to William de Warenne, fig. 15).

To avoid oversimplification we must note certain other variations and complications. The timber tower upon the motte could sometimes stand upon stout posts, as opposed to rising solid from the ground, to enable men to pass beneath it, and thus to provide more space on what is the confined fighting-platform of the motte top. This was the construction of the timber tower upon the motte at Abinger as revealed by

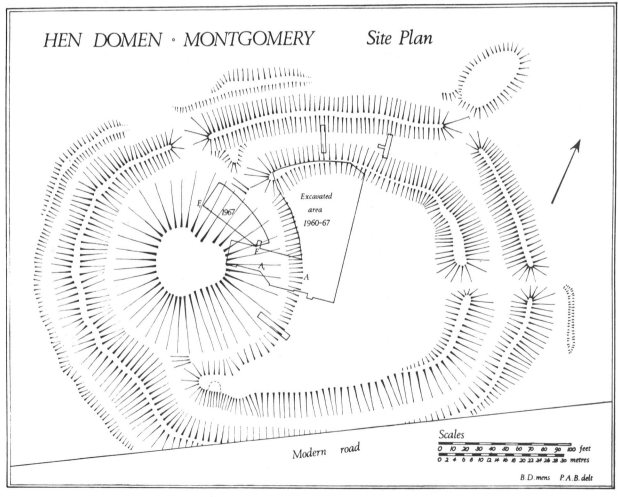

HEN DOMEN · MONTGOMERY   Site Plan

Excavated
area
1960-67

F
1967
E
A₁
A

Modern   road

Scales

0 10 20 30 40 50 60 70 80 90 100 feet

0 2 4 6 8 10 12 14 16 18 20 22 24 26 28 30 metres

B.D. mens   P.A.B. delt

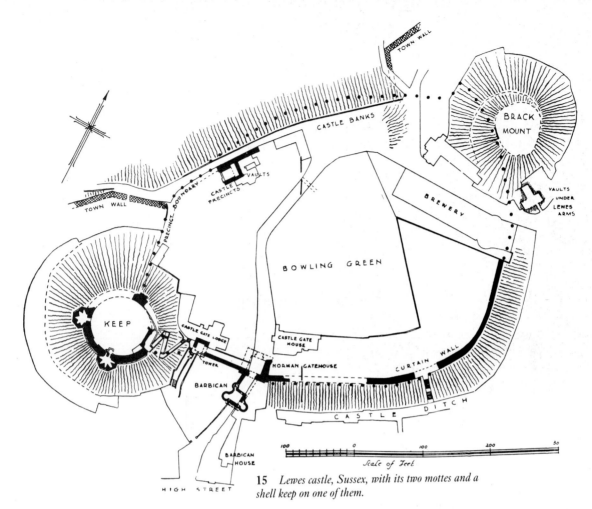

15 *Lewes castle, Sussex, with its two mottes and a shell keep on one of them.*

13 OPPOSITE TOP *The motte (top right), banks and (double) ditches are still the most impressive features of Berkhamsted castle, raised soon after 1066 by the Conqueror's half-brother, Robert, count of Mortain. The ruined shell keep on the motte, the curtain wall of the bailey and the buildings within are later.*

14 OPPOSITE BOTTOM *The currently excavated site of Hen Domen, the original Montgomery castle, raised soon after 1066 in motte-and-bailey form.*

excavation some years ago, as it is evidently also of the tower shown on the motte at Dinan in Brittany on the Bayeux Tapestry. Prior Lawrence likewise wrote of the tower at Durham, 'four posts are plain, one post at each strong corner'. Sometimes, again, it is now known from excavation that the foundations and lower levels of the tower could be built up from the natural ground level with the motte then piled up about them, as was the case at South Mimms and also with the stone tower at Farnham (fig. 16). Such cases are of importance as suggesting that in the minds of contemporaries the tower was, so to speak, the primary element and the motte secondary and defensive to it.

Because of the overwhelming predominance of the motte-and-bailey type amongst early castles in England and Wales dating from the first century after the Norman conquest, because it has been

25

16 *The castle of the bishops of Winchester at Farnham, Surrey. The most interesting feature is the motte (foreground) which excavation showed to have been simply a contemporary adjunct to a twelfth-century tower keep raised up from ground level within it. After the demolition of the tower keep, probably in 1155, the motte was encased in stone to make a very strong shell keep of unusual type.*

archaeologically shown that at Castle Neroche in Somerset the existing motte was added at an early date to a site originally without one, and because it has proved embarrassingly difficult to show that any particular and existing motte in Normandy can be securely dated to the period before 1066, it was recently suggested that this type of castle and the motte itself may have been invented in the unique circumstances of the huge castle-building programme launched in England after the Conquest. The hypothesis was ingenious but cannot stand. There is abundant evidence, not least literary and documentary, to show that the motte was already a familiar feature of castles in northern France, the Rhineland and in Normandy in the first half of the eleventh century. Indeed, there is reason to think that in an age of symbolism, when the castle itself was coming to stand for lordship in men's minds, a particular prestige attached to the motte and its superstructure as the particular and ultimate symbol of lordship. It is

significant that contemporaries could apply to it the word *donjon* which, being derived from the Latin *dominus* meaning lord, means both the dominant feature of a castle and the inner sanctum of lordship. Still used more or less correctly in France, in modern English usage 'donjon' is usually debased to 'dungeon' signifying a close and preferably underground prison, and we have come to prefer 'keep', though that word, oddly enough, does not appear until 1586 in Sidney's *Arcadia*. The Oxford English Dictionary's definition of 'keep', therefore, may equally be applied to 'donjon' in its proper meaning, and would be difficult to improve upon: 'The innermost and strongest structure or central tower of a mediaeval castle, serving as a last defence; a tower, a stronghold, donjon.' (It is interesting to note the OED's illustrative quotation from as late as 1568, 'Come on Sirs, ye shall enter into the dungeon, for then shall ye be sure to be Lordes of the Castell.') So, then, we are told in our contemporary sources that in 1060 Arnold, seneschal of Eustace, count of Boulogne, raised at Ardres (where we have been before) 'a very high motte or lofty donjon', and that in 1026 Eudes II, count of Blois, raised 'a timber tower of marvellous height upon the donjon' of the castle of La-Motte-Montboyau near Tours, and here the word donjon can only mean the motte. The motte was outstandingly the dominant feature of any castle which possessed one, what French architectural historians would call the *pièce maîtresse*, militarily the ultimate strongpoint and at least almost always bearing the particular residence of the castle's lord in the form of a tower rising higher yet. It might itself be revetted in timber or, later, stone, as at South Mimms and Farnham (fig. 16) respectively, to make it more formidable yet. It is worth noting that on the Bayeux Tapestry, made in the second half of the eleventh century, and which uses a kind of architectural shorthand or symbolism to signify its buildings, every castle shown save probably one is represented by its motte alone, while Rouen, the one probable exception, is represented by its great tower of stone which was no less its donjon. One of the most powerful representations of feudal lordship known to me also occurs on the Tapestry in the scene which shows Duke William, the feudal prince, riding into his city of Bayeux. The duke is armed and mounted with his retinue in the full panoply of knighthood; the city is represented by its castle, and the castle by its motte (fig. 12).

ENCLOSURE CASTLES

Nevertheless, it is apparent that many early castles were without mottes, and, indeed, it is possible that the type of castles whose fortification consists only of the ditch, bank and palisade of its enclosure, may be the earliest type of all. It is nowadays fashionable among archaeologists to call such strongholds 'ring works', though the term will be avoided in this book as deeply unsatisfactory. Not only is it clearly absurd (albeit done) to speak of square or rectangular 'ring works' and the like, but the term can or should mean any enclosure of any date, or size, or degree of strength, and so confuses the issue of what is a castle and what is not. That said, the most obvious way to fortify anything, be it city or town containing many distinct buildings, or the various elements – hall, chambers, chapel, stables and the like – of a great man's residence, is to put a defensible enclosure about it. All castles have their fortified enclosures, and the type of castle which consists simply or basically of one or more such enclosures without any motte or great stone tower (though there may be a donjon of some other kind) persists throughout the feudal period from the beginning to the end. Thus in pre-Conquest Normandy, the castle of Le Plessis-Grimoult can be securely dated to before 1047 and has never been altered save by ruin since, because it is known to have been confiscated and slighted in that year as punishment for the rebellion of its lord against the young Duke William and future Conqueror. Developed from an unfortified residence in the early eleventh century, it consisted simply of an enclosure of powerful ditch, bank and (in this case) stone wall, with no motte. Similarly Arques (now Arques-la-Bataille), certainly in existence by 1052 when it was besieged by Duke William, was in the beginning simply an enclosure – though much larger – of ditch and rampart about the residential buildings, perhaps with a timber palisade and gatehouse, perhaps with a curtain wall and gatehouse of stone, before the present stone tower keep was added in the earlier twelfth century by Henry I. The great and prestigious castle of Caen also, founded by the Conqueror himself soon after 1047 as the principal centre of ducal power in Lower Normandy, was in plan merely an enclosure, however vast, though here again fortified from the beginning with a stone curtain wall. Here too, as at Arques, the present stone tower keep was not added until the time of Henry I, though there was always an inner enclosure and sanctum (the donjon?) of palace buildings in which the duke himself had his residence.

In England too, in and after 1066, some of the earliest castles were of the enclosure type. The earliest castle raised here by the Normans, at Pevensey (fig. 1) immediately after their landing, was an enclosure of ditch, bank and presumed palisade cutting off the north-east section of the Old English burgh and former Roman camp (see page 8). Hastings, raised a few days later, evidently had from the beginning a motte which is still there, albeit mutilated, as shown on the Tapestry (fig. 7), but we know of no motte at Dover where the castle planted by the

17 *The triangular-shaped Richmond castle, Yorkshire, stands in an angle of the river Swale. This aerial view (1948) from the west shows the eleventh-century walls, the eleventh-century Scolland's Hall, and the twelfth-century keep, converted from the original gateway, towards the town.*

victorious duke within the surrendered Old English burgh was probably simply an enclosure in the vicinity of the pre-existing Anglo-Saxon church of St Mary and the former Roman lighthouse which served as its bell tower (fig. 51). A parallel case is Old Sarum, where the original and early Norman castle was an enclosure, like a bull's eye in the centre of the Old English burgh and former Iron Age fortress (fig. 3). Even the Conqueror's castle in London, the future 'Tower of London', is now known to have begun as a small enclosure of ditch, bank and presumed palisade in the south-east angle of the city and the Roman walls which still surrounded it (fig. 74). There the insertion of the majestic White Tower – whose dominance has caused the royal castle of London to be called simply the Tower of London ever since – may have been always intended, but an analogy with its first plan is found, for example, at Portchester, where the first castle was an enclosure in the angle of the walled Old English burgh and former Roman camp (fig. 2). Indeed, the cutting-off by bank and ditch and palisade of one corner of a pre-existing larger fortified enclosure, i.e. a town or city, is an obvious type of early castle (the Conqueror's castle at Exeter is

another example, first raised in 1068). Nevertheless, early castles which are basically fortified enclosures without mottes are also found, so to speak, free-standing in the open country. Two which have been recently archaeologically examined are Sulgrave in Northamptonshire and Penmaen in Glamorgan. Neither of these, as it happens, turned out to be very impressive in defensive strength, so that one may wonder how far they ranked as castles (i.e. seriously fortified residences: there is no written reference to either as a castle), but there is no doubt that the enclosure type of castle, without motte or the equivalent of a great tower or tower keep, is a constant in medieval military architecture in England as elsewhere, as witness Richmond (fig. 17) and Ludlow (fig. 18) at the beginning of the century (in both cases the present keeps are twelfth-century additions) or Conway (figs. 80 and 81) and Caernarvon (figs. 84 and 85) towards the end.

MASONRY CASTLES

If not all early castles conformed to the motte-and-bailey plan, so also not all the earliest castles, either on the Continent or later in England, were constructed exclusively of earthwork and timber. Stone building and masonry fortification is there from the beginning, as indeed we should expect of the works of men who were, especially from the tenth century onwards, raising increasingly ambitious and sophisticated churches in stone, and who, in any case, had inherited stone buildings and walled towns and cities from their Carolingian as well as their Roman past.

Original masonry survives at the two earliest known castle sites in Europe and in France, at Doué-la-Fontaine and Langeais (figs. 5 and 6). In pre-conquest Normandy the ramparts of Le Plessis-Grimoult were crowned with a curtain wall, strengthened by mural towers and pierced by a stone gatehouse, before 1047, and the Conqueror's great castle at Caen (like the town itself) was similarly enclosed from the beginning soon after 1047, and with a similar gatehouse which has been revealed by recent excavations. Furthermore a considerable number of early castles in both northern France and Normandy had a stone-built

18 *Ludlow, whose foundation is attributed to Roger de Lacy soon after the Conquest, was from the beginning a stone-built walled and towered enclosure. The two left-hand of the three towers shown are original: the great tower or keep (centre) is the later conversion of the early gatehouse.*

19 *Montbazon (Indre-et-Loire) has one of the earliest rectangular, stone tower keeps in France, generally attributed to Fulk Nerra, count of Anjou, before 1006. The bronze statue of the Virgin was unhappily erected on the north-east angle in 1866.*

great tower – or, as we would now say, tower keep – which, indeed, existed in embryonic form both at Doué-la-Fontaine and Langeais from the beginning. Elsewhere the surviving great towers of Montbazon (fig. 19), Nogent-le-Rotrou and Mondoubleau are all dated to the first half of the eleventh century by French historians, and the list of such early keeps could of course be extended. In Normandy we hear of great towers from the mid-tenth century onwards, at Rouen, Bayeux, Brionne and Ivry. At Ivry, Aubrey, wife of count Raoul d'Ivry, is said to have beheaded the architect, called Lanfred, so that he could not build a similar castle for anyone else (in telling the story, Ordericus Vitalis names another great tower which the unfortunate Lanfred had previously built at Pithiviers). The great tower at Rouen, built by Duke Richard I about 950, may have later served as the model for William the Conqueror's White Tower at London (fig. 9). So, too, in Norman England we find stone building from the beginning, or as soon after as the urgency of the beginning could allow. Merely to cite examples, Richmond and Ludlow (figs. 17 and 18) were evidently enclosed with a stone curtain wall set with mural towers and a gateway (in both cases converted into a tower keep in the twelfth century) from a date soon after 1066, while at Exeter the stone gatehouse of the Conqueror's castle, founded in 1068, still survives (fig. 56). The great tower of stone, the tower keep, also appears in England in the first generation of the Norman settlement, most notably at the Tower of London (fig. 9), but also at Colchester (fig. 22) and Chepstow (fig. 54).

TOWER KEEPS

Though often associated particularly and almost exclusively with the twelfth century, when it was certainly very popular, it is clear that the tower keep was a feature of many castles in all periods. Nor is this surprising, for if a large, strong and defensible house is required one method of achieving it, scarcely less fundamental than enclosure, is to bring all the necessary elements – storerooms, state rooms, chambers, chapel – together into one integrated unit and the result is likely to be a tower and high-rise living. Add medieval symbolism and the architectural expression of lordly dominance and one has in the great stone tower the donjon *par excellence* dominating the countryside and the castle which possesses this feature, at once the military strongpoint of the whole fortress and containing the more privy apartments of the lord and his immediate entourage. The great tower of stone is the equivalent of the motte with its timber tower: both are types of donjon performing the same function, real and symbolic; and the fact that the stone tower usually needed no motte to protect

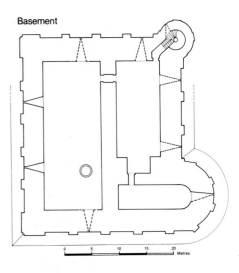

Basement

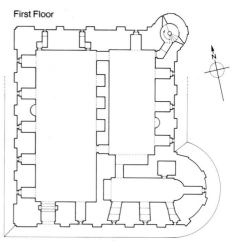

First Floor

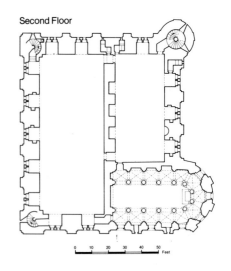

Second Floor

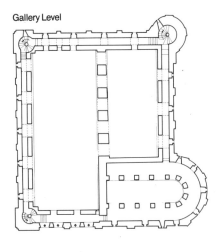

Gallery Level

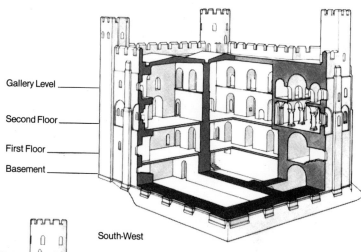

20 *The White Tower (c. 1100), floor plans. As built there were only two residential floors above the basement, the second (for the king) rising through two storeys with a gallery. The Chapel of St John is at second-floor level. Cf. fig. 21.*

Gallery Level

Second Floor

First Floor

Basement

South-West

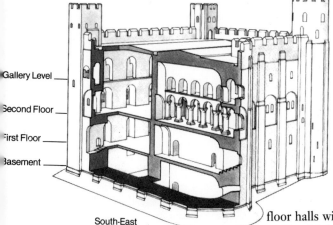

Gallery Level

Second Floor

First Floor

Basement

South-East

21 *Cut-away drawings of the White Tower in the Norman period.*

further the immense strength of its splayed out base, combined with the increasing fashion for building in stone, no doubt explains why the motte does not survive as a feature of new castles built after, say, the mid-twelfth century. But the stone tower keep does thus survive, and, contrary to what is sometimes said, there is really no difference in concept between the great tower built at Tattershall (fig. 47) in the fifteenth century and Rochester (fig. 28) or Newcastle-on-Tyne built in the twelfth – or, one may add, the Conqueror's White Tower at London (fig. 9).

Some of these earliest stone tower keeps, notably Langeais (fig. 6), are of no great height but are in essence very strong first-

floor halls with a basement below the single residential floor, and are thus comparatively squat and oblong in outline, as opposed to towers proper, rising through three or more storeys. Brionne in Normandy was evidently of this type in 1047 as William of Poitiers later described it: 'This castle, both by the manner of its construction and the nature of the site, seemed impregnable. For in addition to the other fortifications which the needs of war require, it has a stone-built hall serving the defenders as a keep.' In England, Chepstow (fig. 54), dating from the Conqueror's reign, was obviously similar, consisting only of a basement and one residential floor before its thirteenth-century heightening, and the type persisted in such later keeps as Norwich (fig. 27), Falaise or Castle Rising (fig. 25). The Tower of London itself (fig. 9 and figs. 20, 21), though

22 *Like the White Tower, i.e. the 'Tower of London', than which it is even bigger, the great keep at Colchester in Essex (its upper stages demolished in the seventeenth century) was built or begun by William the Conqueror. These two towers are the most impressive architectural expression of Norman secular rule in England. They are similar in plan, including the apse of the chapel projecting at the south-east angle.*

three storeys high, has something of this nature, derived ultimately, as it is thought to be, from the great Carolingian halls and palaces of the past. Though scarcely squat, it is formidable rather than lofty, and shares with the Conqueror's other great keep at Colchester (fig. 22) the otherwise unique feature of an apsidal projection at one angle (the south-east) which houses the apse of the chapel. Colchester is even bigger than the White Tower (110 x 151½ ft as opposed to 107 x 118 ft) but follows very much the same plan, though it is now partly ruined, having lost its upper stages from attempted demolition after the seventeenth-century Civil War, while its internal features are obscured by the museum which it houses.

There is nothing else quite like these two great buildings anywhere else in Western Europe (and therefore in the world), and the White Tower, which still stands complete, above all gives some impression of the power of eleventh-century Normandy and the

regality of the first Norman king of England. It stands 90 ft high to the battlements with four corner turrets rising above, and its walls are of immense thickness, varying from 12 ft to 15 ft at the base where they rise from a splayed out or 'battered' plinth on three sides. The entrance (recently restored) was where it is now, at first-floor level on the south side. Internally, the building consisted of a basement and two residential floors (not three as now), of which the second, served by the intensely Norman chapel of St John (fig. 10), was much the grander, rising through two storeys with a mural gallery about it, and clearly intended for the king himself. Vertically from top to bottom the great tower is divided by a cross wall placed more or less centrally, to provide greater structural rigidity and support the roof, thus affording at each level two principal apartments which on the residential floors are great hall and great chamber. Each residential floor is well supplied with fireplaces and garderobes, and a vice or spiral staircase in the north-east angle turret provides communication between each level.

4 The Development of the Castle

The early castle, in England let us say from *c.*1066 to *c.*1100, whatever building materials it employed, already showed the basic principles of design which remain for the rest of the Middle Ages. The enclosure, of course, was there, and so was the great tower. Lesser towers were employed to strengthen walls, with already a particular and necessary concentration on the gateway as a potential weak point, usually by incorporating it in a strong tower pierced by the entrance passage. Most of these techniques, after all, were inherited from the classical and Roman past, though the concept of the donjon and its expression as motte or great tower are best thought of as peculiar to the medieval and feudal periods. Thenceforth the development of the castle will be largely a matter of details and the increasingly sophisticated application of techniques known and inherited, until that unique combination of lordly residence and fortress which makes a castle slowly splits asunder, and castles cease to be built save as consciously antiquarian exercises. This development will differ little as between England or Britain and the continent, especially France, for the medieval world of Latin Christendom was a unity and its society largely universal in its customs, concepts, needs and aspirations.

There is a continuity of architectural development in castles which thus differs from the development of ecclesiastical architecture. The stylistic changes which we are taught to see in the latter scarcely apply to castles, nor do such labels as 'Early English' or 'Perpendicular', and certainly there is no dramatic transition in medieval military architecture from one method of building which we call 'Romanesque' to another called 'Gothic'. The time-scale of the development of castles is different from that of churches, and when the Romanesque church reached its apogee at Durham or Lessay at the close of the eleventh century to be replaced by the Gothic churches of St Denis or Chartres, castles still had two centuries of continuous and consistent development to reach such high points as Caernarvon (fig. 84) or Beaumaris (fig. 86), Conway (fig. 80) or Harlech (fig. 82). One tends to forget how far the terminology of medieval architectural history has come exclusively from ecclesiastical architecture. Who, after all, has ever heard of, let alone seen, a Romanesque or Decorated castle?

Another point leading to continuity in the architectural development of castles is that in England and Wales certainly – and doubtless elsewhere if a study were made – the great majority of castles were of early foundation, so that the typical architectural history of the typical English or Welsh castle is of continuous development on the same site. We should certainly note that so great was the number of castles raised in the first century after the Norman Conquest – the first century of English feudalism, let us say – that thereafter the total number of castles in the realm declines, as the cost of increasingly elaborate building in stone increases (there was also inflation in the second half of the twelfth century wholly comparable to that of

33

our own day) and the particular pressures of the Norman Conquest and settlement declined. Thereafter new castles on new sites are the exception, and call for a particular explanation from the historian.

The building of new castles to hold down new territories acquired is one such explanation, and Edward I's great castles planted in and about Gwynedd and north Wales – Flint (fig. 78) and Rhuddlan (fig. 79), Conway (fig. 80) and Caernarvon (fig. 84), Harlech (fig. 82) and Beaumaris (fig. 86) – are splendid illustrations of it. (Part and parcel as they are of Edward's conquest of Wales, it is a sloppy misuse of language and a standing of history on its head to call them 'Welsh' castles.) The endemic warfare, raids and counter-raids in the Scottish Marches, which follow the same Edward's un-successful attempt to conquer Scotland for the rest of the Middle Ages and beyond, provide a different reason for new fortification in the north of England in the later medieval centuries. Other reasons may be less dramatic. Castles, as lordly residences and an ostentation of nobility, are often more personal than national, and building on the grand scale may be a personal affair. New castles may express new lordship simply in the social sense. Thus in 1138 the young William of Albini II married Alice 'the queen', i.e the second wife and young widow of King Henry I, and, at a stroke, went very near the top of the close-knit Anglo-Norman aristocracy. It was said that he became so puffed-up as to look down on everyone save the new king (Stephen) himself, and he gave grandiloquent expression to his new eminence by building in Norfolk, where his patrimony was, two new castles, New Buckenham and Castle Rising (fig. 27).

THE SHELL KEEP

As from the twelfth century, a natural and increasing preference for the greater strength and sophistication of stone building, together with the increasing fashion in that century for a donjon in the form of a great stone tower, i.e. the tower keep, presumably accounts for the decline of the motte in the sense that fewer and fewer new ones were raised. Nevertheless, those very many castles in England and Wales which had begun with a motte were likely to be stuck with it in the pre-bulldozer age, or their lords attached to it as an undoubted sign of ancient nobility.

If one wished to replace the timber superstructures of a motte with masonry it was easy enough to build a ring wall about its summit instead of the former palisade, but less easy to replace the timber tower within by a great tower of stone on the potentially weak foundation of an artifical mound. It could, of course, be done, as it was with the great tower on the great motte at Norwich (fig. 26), while at Clun (fig 23) and Guildford a safe compromise was achieved by building the tower up and into the side of the mound so that its foundations were on ground level. The combination of tower keep (especially perhaps a cylindrical tower which fits rather better) and ring wall on top of a motte is not in fact uncommon, as at Launceston (fig. 25), Tretower (fig. 36), Mitford or Norham (or Gisors in Normandy), and is in fact the straight translation into masonry of the timber superstructure of an earlier phase. Nevertheless there seems plenty of evidence to show that very often, and perhaps usually, the masonry development of a motte produced simply the ring wall about its summit, with no great tower within it but ranges of residential apartments for the lord and his immediate household disposed about the inner face of the wall and of one build with it. A classic surviving example of this arrangement is to be found at Restormel in Cornwall (fig. 24), often attributed in its completion to Richard, earl of Cornwall, in the thirteenth century, and 'houses' upon the motte, i.e. within its surviving ring wall, were built for Henry II at Berkhamsted (fig. 13) in the later twelfth. There are in fact innumerable surviving examples of what archaeologists call the 'shell keep'. It was indeed a form of keep or donjon as the motte with its timber superstructure had been before it, the dominant feature of the castle, its ultimate strongpoint, and the privy residence of its lord. That it could be grand enough for this practical and symbolic role is indicated, to take one small instance, by the splendidly decorated entrance to the now gutted shell keep on the motte at Arundel (fig. 102), built, we may suppose, by William of Albini II when he acquired the castle by

his marriage to Alice 'the queen' in 1138 (see page 34). At royal Windsor (fig. 88) the shell keep (heightened and altered by 'restoration' in the early nineteenth century), raised probably by Henry I upon the motte of the Conqueror, his father, was fitted out by Edward III in the fourteenth century with a sumptuous range of timber-framed apartments which are still there. At Farnham (fig. 16) and at Berkeley there is a variant arrangement whereby the ring wall, instead of being built like a crown about the summit, rises from the base of the motte to revet it in stone and thus present a seemingly impregnable obstacle to the foe. Elsewhere and often the so-called shell keep might be strengthened by mural towers (one perhaps serving as a gate tower) on or about its circuit, as is the case at Lewes (fig. 15), Restormel

23 *At the Fitz Alan castle of Clun, Shropshire, the twelfth-century tower keep was built into the side of the earlier motte so that its foundations could rest on the natural ground level.*

24 *An aerial view of Restormel in Cornwall affords a classic, textbook example of a shell keep. The bailey of the castle has almost vanished, but a crenellated ring wall of c. 1200 stands about the summit of the earlier motte. The residential buildings within – hall, chambers, kitchen, chapel – date from the late thirteenth century and are attributed either to Richard or Edmund his son, successively earls of Cornwall.*

25 *At Launceston in Cornwall the accumulated later stonework upon the huge original motte – thirteenth-century mantlet wall, twelfth-century 'shell keep' and thirteenth-century great tower – made a formidable donjon to symbolize the lordship of Richard earl of Cornwall, Henry III's brother, whose castle it was in the thirteenth century.*

(fig. 24) or Tamworth, Arundel (fig. 102), Carisbrooke or Berkhamsted (fig. 13). Sometimes, indeed, a whole complex of motte, shell, towers and residential buildings could be developed into an imposing donjon as formidable and forbidding as any tower keep be it never so grand; one thinks of the complex at Launceston (fig. 25) or the Seven Towers of the Percies at Alnwick, or the lordly edifice now revealed by excavation at Sandal, with flanking towers, projecting gatehouse and barbican trust out in front again

THE TOWER KEEP

Meanwhile that form of donjon which is the tower keep underwent considerable development, not least in the course of the twelfth century when it was especially in fashion. One development which may as well be separately noted first is the forebuilding, generally absent in the earliest examples. Its function is to cover the entrance to the keep, itself almost invariably placed at first-floor level for obvious security reasons. The forebuilding is thus a kind of annexe, consisting of one or more towers through which the necessary external stairway passes, containing an entrance vestibule, and often a chapel, in the extra space thus provided. Such a feature is lacking at Chepstow (fig. 55) and the Tower of London, though the latter undoubtedly had one added later (probably in the twelfth century) which has now disappeared again as the result of the savage demolitions which took place there from the late seventeenth century onwards, when the proud castle ceased to be a royal residence (fig. 9, cf. fig. 104). By contrast, Henry II's great tower at Dover, built a century later and the ultimate in England of the rectangular tower keep, has as an integral part of its structure what is fittingly one of the grandest and most elaborate forebuildings in the kingdom, its stairway ascending two

26 *Restored and refaced with the wrong stone in the nineteenth century, the great tower keep at Norwich is nevertheless remarkable for the elaborate decoration of blind arcading upon its upper stories. Standing on the motte of the Conqueror's castle, it is attributed to Henry I, though the basement level may be earlier. In plan it resembles Castle Rising (fig. 27) and Falaise.*

sides of the keep through three subsidiary towers (fig. 32).

The type of tower keep already noted at Langeais (fig. 6) and Chepstow (fig. 54), more oblong than vertical and evidently derived from the first-floor hall, persists in the twelfth century, notably at Middleham and Kenilworth, Norwich (fig. 26) and Castle Rising (fig. 27). The last two both have close affinities with Falaise in Normandy and with each other. Norwich, like Falaise, is attributed, at least in its final form, to Henry I, and Rising was built soon after 1138 by William of Albini II, doubtless as a copy of Norwich in honour of his wife. Both had very similar forebuildings with grand entrance vestibules at first-floor level. That at Rising survives more or less complete, though altered and its splendid doorway into the keep proper now blocked. Norwich is badly mutilated (even its present floor levels are wrong), having long served as a prison and now being heavily disguised as a museum, but at Rising, though its roof and floors are gone, the original arrangement, reflecting that at Norwich, can be clearly seen. There were only two principal storeys, namely a basement and one residential floor above – in French parlance, *étage noble* – though there is one isolated chamber at a higher level above the chapel. The residential floor, however, is much more elaborate than the single great apartment or great hall at Chepstow, and consists of great hall and great chamber, respectively on either side of the cross-wall, with a fine chapel adjacent to the great chamber, and a kitchen and service room adjacent to the great hall. Each of the principal apartments has the necessary garderobe facilities contrived in the thickness of the walls, those serving the great chamber having every appearance of being separately designed 'Ladies' and 'Gentlemen' – perhaps the first known instance of this nicety in England.

27 *The rectangular tower keep at Castle Rising in Norfolk was the principal building and strength of the new castle raised (together with New Buckenham) in c. 1140 by William of Albini II to celebrate his marriage to Alice 'the queen', young widow of Henry I, and his consequent acquisition of the earldom of Sussex. It was modelled on the keep at Norwich (fig. 26), attributed to Henry I.*

The great towers proper, whose principal dimension is the vertical, are, however, in the ascendant in France and in Normandy (e.g. Arques, Caen, Domfront, Brionne, all dating from the earlier twelfth century) as well as in England and Wales. As a specimen we may take the classic case of Rochester (figs. 28-30), though noting that this has close affinities with the keep at Castle Hedingham in Essex, belonging to the Vere earl of Oxford, and evidently built about the same time and very much to the same plan. The tower keep at Rochester, we know, is the 'noble tower' built by Archbishop William de Corbeil, to whom and his successors at Canterbury the king had granted the perpetual custody of the castle, with permission to make 'a fortification or tower within · the castle and keep and hold it forever'. (The custody of the royal castle of Rochester by the archbishops of Canterbury was later broken by an enraged King John when Archbishop Stephen Langton had handed the fortress over to the king's enemies in 1215 after Magna Carta.) The tower was thus added in the earlier twelfth century to a castle which had begun simply as an enclosure soon after 1066 and had been rebuilt in stone by Gundulf, bishop of Rochester, for William Rufus. It survives complete save for a small part of its forebuilding, and its roof and floors whose absence makes it difficult now for the visitor to envisage the former splendour of its interior. It measures 70 ft square (cf. therefore Colchester and the Tower of London) and rises from a battered plinth 113 ft to the parapet and a further 12 ft to the tops of its corner turrets. Its strength is immense though largely passive, its walls 12 ft thick at the base, narrowing to 10 ft at the summit. It has or had an elaborate forebuilding arrangement whereby the external stairway rose against two faces of the keep, through a small defensive turret at the north-east angle and so up to the main forebuilding tower, entered across a drawbridge pit into a grand entrance vestibule at first-floor level. Above this in the forebuilding tower there is a chapel and, below, a basement. The great tower itself is divided internally east-west and top to bottom by a cross-wall, a normal feature of the larger rectangular tower keeps,

here placed centrally. At Rochester there were three residential floors above a basement, joined by two grand spiral staircases, respectively in the north-west and south-east turrets, and each divided into two main apartments, one on either side of the cross-wall and with an additional small chamber in the north-east angle. On the first and second residential floors the two main apartments presumably served as the two basic essentials of medieval aristocratic life, great hall and great chamber. The second residential suite is clearly the grander, intended for the lord of the castle himself. As at the Tower of London, it rises through two levels with a mural gallery, and here on this floor the cross-wall is pierced by a grand and decorated round-arched arcade. The intended function of the third and top-most residential floor is less certain, but it has or had, as befits an episcopal keep, another and a grand chapel in the eastern half of its southern division. Perhaps, therefore, it provided the privy apartments of the archbishop as opposed to the state apartments (for the king if necessary?) immediately below.

Two more features of the keep at Rochester remain to be noted. For greater convenience the shaft of the well, placed centrally, is brought up through the cross-wall to each floor where there is a well-head in each case. Also above the roof line there is a double row of pigeon holes along the inner face of the north wall – as there were many others now blocked in the corner turrets – to remind us, like the dovecotes of ancient manors, of a further aspect of lordly domestic economy in the past. Indeed, with its empty but evocative fireplaces and careful provision of garderobes (it is Louis XIV's Versailles and the elegant palaces of the Age of Reason, not the residences of our medieval kings and princes, which make do with chamberpots), the donjon of Rochester still reveals its residential function in spite of its forlorn and bleak internal appearance now, all comfort,

28 *Built by archbishop William de Corbeil in c. 1127 within the existing castle, the keep at Rochester is one of the earliest and finest great towers in the kingdom. It has a basement and three residential floors, and a forebuilding (left) covers the entrance at first-floor level.*

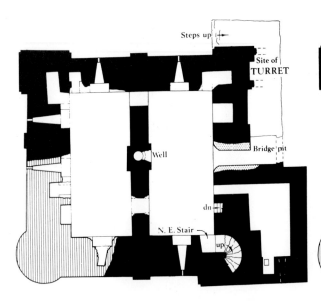

GROUND FLOOR (BASEMENT)

FIRST FLOOR

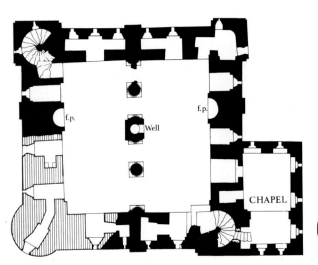

SECOND (PRINCIPAL) FLOOR

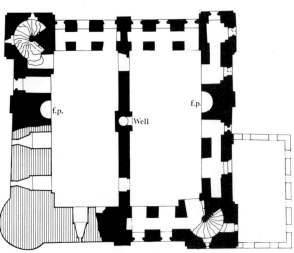

THIRD (TOP) FLOOR

■ Begun 1127

▥ Rebuilt 1226–7

▦ Later

29 *Rochester castle: floor plans of the keep. The huge damage done
by John's mine in 1215 can be seen in the rebuilt sections.*

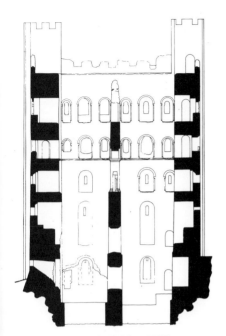

SECTION LOOKING WEST

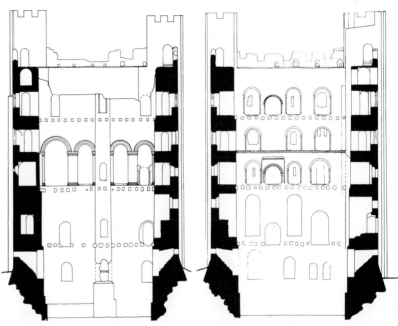

SECTION THROUGH NORTH PART
LOOKING SOUTH

SECTION THROUGH NORTH PART
LOOKING NORTH

SECTION LOOKING EAST

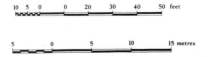

30 *Rochester castle: elevations of the keep.*

furnishings and hangings gone. It also shows like all donjons that unique combination of lordly residence and military purpose which is the peculiar characteristic of castles and each of their several parts. The portcullis defending the doorway into the entrance vestibule of the forebuilding was worked from the chapel above, and about the summit of the great tower itself one may still see the holes or sockets for the joists of the 'hoarding' or 'brattice' – a projecting timber gallery fitted to protect the base of the building in time of war (fig. 49). The strength and defences of Rochester were needed, for the castle's dramatic military history contains three sieges, in 1088, 1215 and 1264. In the second of these, King John, having broken into the bailey, set his miners at the keep, one huge section of which, in the south-eastern quarter, was brought down (see p. 113). The repair of the damage after the war can still be seen, externally in the cylindrical rebuilding of the south-east angle, and internally especially at the top level, where the decoration of the upper chapel has not been properly replaced.

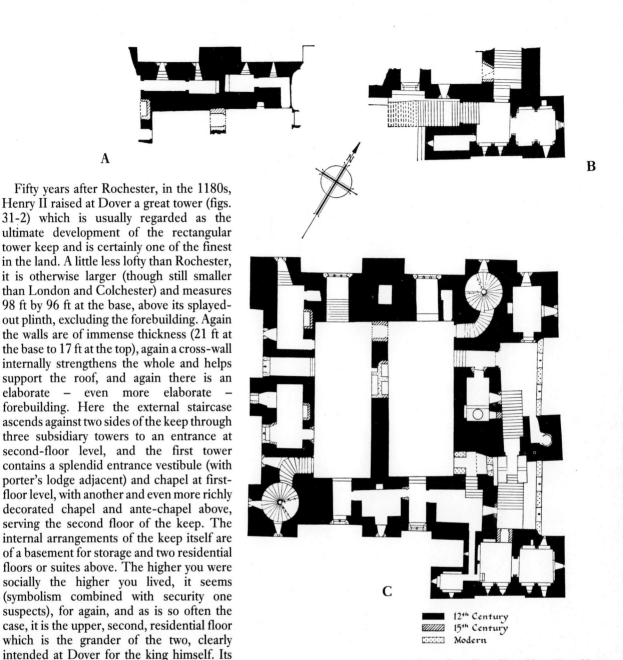

A

B

C

Fifty years after Rochester, in the 1180s, Henry II raised at Dover a great tower (figs. 31-2) which is usually regarded as the ultimate development of the rectangular tower keep and is certainly one of the finest in the land. A little less lofty than Rochester, it is otherwise larger (though still smaller than London and Colchester) and measures 98 ft by 96 ft at the base, above its splayed-out plinth, excluding the forebuilding. Again the walls are of immense thickness (21 ft at the base to 17 ft at the top), again a cross-wall internally strengthens the whole and helps support the roof, and again there is an elaborate – even more elaborate – forebuilding. Here the external staircase ascends against two sides of the keep through three subsidiary towers to an entrance at second-floor level, and the first tower contains a splendid entrance vestibule (with porter's lodge adjacent) and chapel at first-floor level, with another and even more richly decorated chapel and ante-chapel above, serving the second floor of the keep. The internal arrangements of the keep itself are of a basement for storage and two residential floors or suites above. The higher you were socially the higher you lived, it seems (symbolism combined with security one suspects), for again, and as is so often the case, it is the upper, second, residential floor which is the grander of the two, clearly intended at Dover for the king himself. Its grandeur ruined now by the hideous 'bomb-proof arches' inserted in *c.* 1800 to enable heavy guns to be mounted on the roof against the threat of Napoleon's invasion, it rose like the principal floor at London, Rochester and Castle Hedingham through two stages with a

■ 12th Century
▨ 15th Century
▧ Modern

10 0 10 20 30 40 50
    Scale of Feet

5 0 5 10 15
    Scale of Metres

31 OPPOSITE *The great rectangular tower keep of Henry II at Dover. Most of the window openings date from 'modernization' in the fifteenth century.*

32 *Dover, plan of keep. (A) garderobes in the north wall; (B) forebuilding at first-floor level; (C) keep at second-floor level. The forebuilding covering the entrance stands east and south of the main tower.*

43

33 *The unusual-looking shape of the donjon at Houdan (Yvelines) in the Ile de France in fact consists of a cylindrical tower with four semi-circular buttress-turrets. It is attributed to Amaury III, count of Montfort, between 1110 and 1125, and now serves shamefully as a municipal water-tower.*

still showing his badge of the rose 'en soleil' in their spandrels. Internal communication between each level of the keep is provided by two broad vices or spiral staircases diametrically opposite each other in the north-east and south-west angle turrets. In a manner reminiscent of Rochester, the well shaft is brought up to the top floor of the keep, but here there is a sophisticated difference. The well-chamber, on the left of the passage leading into the royal apartments from the forebuilding at second-floor level, contains not only the well-head, but also a recessed basin or sink in which lead pipes can still be seen leading off to other parts of the keep. In other words, the donjon at Dover had a piped water supply in the late twelfth century.

The keep at Dover has close affinities with another of Henry II's great towers at Newcastle-upon-Tyne, which is rather smaller (62 ft by 56 ft) but is known to have been built a few years earlier, between 1172 and 1177, and by the same master mason, who appears on the Pipe Rolls as Maurice the Engineer. Henry II, indeed, like his grandfather Henry I, was a mighty builder of rectangular tower keeps, responsible for Scarborough, Bridgenorth and the Peak (at Castleton) as well as Newcastle and Dover, and partly responsible (in that he completed them) for those of Bamburgh, Bowes and Richmond (fig. 17). He also built the rather different types of tower to be found at Orford, Chilham and Tickhill (figs. 40-2) but, before we turn to those, no list of the characteristically rectangular great towers of the twelfth century can be allowed to close without a mention – in roughly chronological order, some royal and some baronial – of Castle Acre (enigmatic and perhaps earlier), Canterbury and Corfe, Carlisle and Portchester, Bungay and Norham.

Characteristic as these great buildings are of the twelfth century, they are nevertheless not confined to that century, but occur both earlier and later, and during the course of that century, in France especially but also in Wales and England, there was much experiment to produce tower keeps of some other shape than rectangular. In France the cylindrical donjons of Fréteval and Château-sur-Epte are both dated to the first half of the

mural gallery about it at the upper level to give more lofty space and light. This floor has also the finer of the two chapels. Each floor is divided by the cross-wall into two large apartments serving respectively as great hall (east?) and great chamber (west?), while the thickness of the walls enables a number of lesser and mural chambers to be provided, presumably for sleeping. That situated in the north-west corner of the second floor, with fireplace and private access to its own garderobe, is thought to have been the bedchamber of the king. Both residential floors are properly provided with garderobes and fireplaces, the latter (like most of the doorways and the window openings of the keep) now fifteenth-century in appearance, having been 'modernized' for Edward IV and twelfth century, as are the more sophisticatedly or more curiously shaped Houdan (fig. 33) and Etampes, the former cylindrical with cylindrical buttresses and the latter quadrilobe. Perhaps the most dramatic of the experimentally shaped tower keeps, evidently in vogue at the turn of the twelfth and thirteenth centuries, are those *en bec* or beaked, three-quarters round but with a prow of solid masonry pointing in the direction from which attack is most expected. La Tour Blanche at Issoudun (fig. 34) is a splendid example, raised *c.* 1202 by King Philip II 'Augustus'. Richard I's remarkable donjon at Château-Gaillard (1196-8), on the Seine and the borders of Normandy then under attack from King Philip, is a more sophisticated version of the same type, with a machicolated warhead (now gone – for machicolation see fig. 50) borne on wedge-shaped corbels fanning out from its circumference (figs. 75-6), and a more primitive version from which Château-Gaillard may be derived stands a little further upstream at La Roche Guyon, attributed to Philip in *c.* 1190. In general, however, Philip 'Augustus', the eventual conqueror of Normandy and much more of the Angevin dominions in France from John, king of England, seems to have preferred the great cylindrical donjons, which over and over again he planted in the castles of the lands he won, evidently as a sign and symbol of his new lordship. Amongst others the round tower keeps at Dourdan and Châteaudun, Falaise and Verneuil, Lillebonne, Gisors, Rouen, are all attributed to him. Greatest of all the cylindrical donjons, however, was the now vanished tower at Coucy-le-Château built by Enguerrand III, lord of Coucy, also in the earlier thirteenth century.

Cylindrical tower keeps are fewer in the English kingdom, and, for that matter, in the French dominions of the kings of England before the conquests of Philip II in 1204. They are principally confined, indeed, to Wales and the Marches at the turn of the twelfth and thirteenth centuries, as witness the splendid examples at Pembroke (fig. 35) and Tretower (fig. 36), or Bronllys, Longtown and Skenfrith. There are, however, notable exceptions. A great cylindrical tower stands on the motte at

34 *La Tour Blanche at Issoudun (Indre). The donjon of the castle is c.1202 and in the latest French fashion, en bec, i.e. here a cylindrical great tower with a solid prow facing the line of attack. The holes for hoarding (cf. fig. 49) about the summit are clearly visible.*

Launceston (early to mid-thirteenth century, and by Richard, earl of Cornwall, fig. 25); Conisbrough (figs. 37 and 40) has a cylindrical tower with thrusting wedge-shaped buttresses (*c.* 1180 and Warenne); and the little-known New Buckenham in Norfolk, now a mere ruin, dates from soon after 1138 (the marriage of William of Albini once again). Henry III's Wakefield Tower at the Tower of London (fig. 38), recently restored and containing that king's privy chamber in its upper storey, is or was really an English version of the French *donjon cylindrique*, though everything at the Tower is subsidiary to the White Tower of the Conqueror.

35 OPPOSITE TOP *Though founded in the late eleventh century, Pembroke as we see it now, discounting restoration, is almost entirely the work of the Marshal earls of Pembroke a century and more later. The deliberately dominant feature, shown here, is the great cylindrical tower keep of that date.*

36 OPPOSITE BOTTOM *Tretower in Breconshire shows its strength with a splendid cylindrical tower-keep of early thirteenth-century date and a 'shell keep' wrapped close about it, the two making a formidable donjon.*

37 RIGHT TOP *The present castle at Conisbrough, Yorkshire, is almost entirely the work of earl Hamelin Plantagenet, half-brother of Henry II, between c. 1180 and 1200. The formidable tower keep is cylindrical with the addition of six wedge-shaped solid buttresses. Cf. fig. 40.*

38 RIGHT BOTTOM *Cut-away drawings of the Wakefield Tower, c. 1225, at the Tower of London. Note the construction of the timber ceiling at first-floor level. The room above was Henry III's privy chamber.*

There is no known version of the donjon *en bec* in the English kingdom, though the exciting shape occurs in certain of the mural towers (Norfolk and Fitzwilliam) at Dover built in the early thirteenth century (fig. 51). There was evidently no quadrilobe or quatrefoil shape either until Henry III built the unique specimen on the Conqueror's motte at York (fig. 39), though Pontefract had a trefoil tower keep in the same thirteenth century. There is, however, a small stylistic group of polygonal great towers (fig. 40), widely distributed about the country, at Chilham, Orford, Tickhill, Richard's Castle and Odiham, all dating from the late twelfth and early thirteenth centuries and the first three attributed to Henry II. To them we should also add Gisors in Normandy which is also his. Of all these the most impressive and the most complete is Orford (figs. 41-2) on the Suffolk coast, built between 1165 and, probably, 1167, at a cost of just under £1000. Standing 90 ft high from a battered plinth, with walls 10 ft thick, in shape it is octagonal with the addition of three buttress-towers and a forebuilding.

39 *The mid-thirteenth-century Clifford's Tower at York, an unusual quadrilobe shape in plan, stands on the original motte of one of the two castles raised in the city by William the Conqueror in 1068 and 1070.*

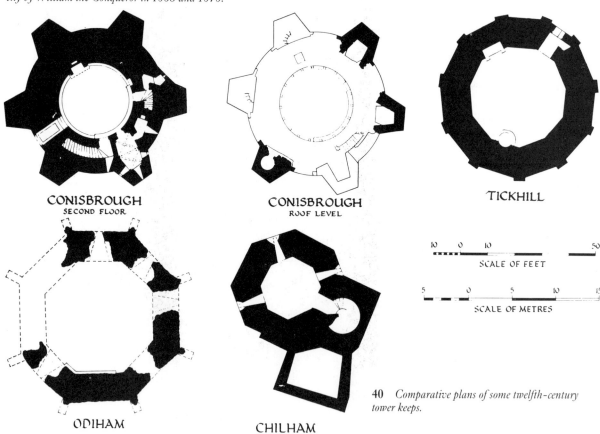

CONISBROUGH
SECOND FLOOR

CONISBROUGH
ROOF LEVEL

TICKHILL

ODIHAM

CHILHAM

10   0   10   50
SCALE OF FEET

5   0   5   10   15
SCALE OF METRES

40 *Comparative plans of some twelfth-century tower keeps.*

41 *The tower-keep, long preserved as a landmark for shipping, is all that remains upstanding of Henry II's castle at Orford on the Suffolk coast, built between 1165 and 1173. It is of unusual design, a polygonal tower with three rectangular buttress towers and the forebuilding housing the entrance. Cf. fig. 42.*

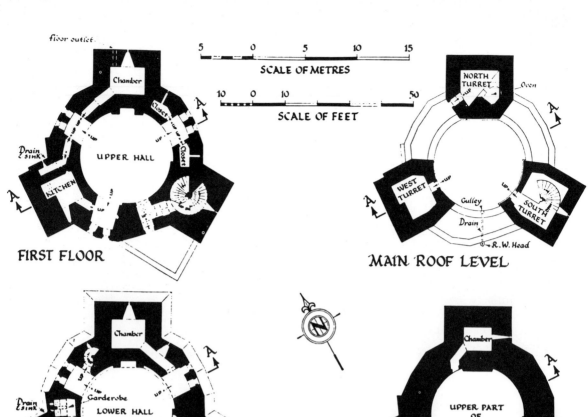

FIRST FLOOR

MAIN ROOF LEVEL

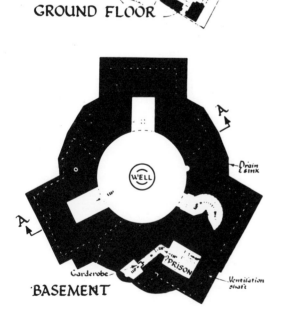

GROUND FLOOR

MEZZANINE
FIRST FLOOR & ROOF LEVELS

BASEMENT

MEZZANINE
GROUND & FIRST FLOOR LEVELS

42 *Floor plans of Henry II's tower keep at Orford, Suffolk.*

Internally there are two main residential floors above a basement, and again the upper floor is the grander of the two. Each residential floor or suite has one great cylindrical apartment, i.e. great hall, occupying the entire interior space of the great tower, with a subsidiary chamber and a kitchen in two of the three buttress turrets (the third contains the vice). There is the usual careful provision of fireplaces and garderobes on each floor, and a beautiful small chapel in the upper storey of the forebuilding, with the chaplain's own accommodation adjacent consisting of his chamber and his private garderobe (one of the best preserved twelfth-century examples in the country?).

The experimentation in the shapes of tower keeps in the twelfth and early thirteenth century (the same experimentation is found in mural towers of the period as we shall see) is often attributed to progress. In this view the cylindrical towers, or the towers *en bec*, with the minimum of flat surface to receive head-on the missiles of the foe, and no angles for undermining or to produce dead ground to the defenders, are the ultimate development, while any tower which is not either rectangular or cylindrical is 'transitional'. In fact, however, the known dates of many of

43 *An aerial photograph of Pickering (Yorks.) from the west shows the original motte-and-bailey layout of the castle together with its later stone buildings and defences, including the King's tower or shell keep upon the motte and the fourteenth-century curtain, with rectangular towers, of the barbican or outer bailey above and right.*

the towers under discussion will scarcely allow a near progression from square to round – Henry II built the 'transitional' Orford a decade before the uncompromisingly rectangular Dover, and New Buckenham antedates half the rectangular tower keeps in the country, to make only two obvious points – and that changing fashions, and the perhaps rival theories of individual lords and their master masons, are more the cause of variation than progress leading to a generally accepted superiority of one form over another, seems proved when the rectangular great tower (e.g. Tattershall, fig. 47) and mural tower (e.g. Pickering, fig. 43) reappear in the later Middle Ages. Further, at least half the function of any keep is residential, and whatever military advantages the cylindrical, polygonal and other towers may have had, they scarcely lent themselves to more than one apartment, usually itself cylindrical, on each floor; nor could they easily accommodate the useful adjunct of a forebuilding.

It is sometimes said that not only the rectangular keep but the tower keep itself of

44 *The late fourteenth-century donjon at Nunney in Somerset, which is all that remains of the castle, was always its principal glory and strength. In design it is very French (cf. Pierrefonds, Tarascon, and the Paris Bastille), rectangular with four drum towers at the angles, the whole rising through four storeys with machicolation all round at parapet level.*

whatever shape became obsolete soon after 1200, and that, therefore, Henry II's Dover, for example, was obsolescent when he built it. Setting aside the improbable slight upon a mighty castle-building prince who very much knew what he was doing, one may urge that the tower-keep type of donjon survives triumphantly throughout the feudal period. Those castles which had a great tower of course retained it, commanding the whole edifice as of old, but also new tower keeps, of various shapes, were raised between the thirteenth and the fifteenth centuries – at York (fig. 39) and Pontefract, Flint (fig. 78) and Cambridge, in the thirteenth century; at Knaresborough, Dudley, Nunney (fig. 44), Southampton, Dunstanburgh, Old Wardour and the remarkable Warkworth (figs. 45-6) in the fourteenth century; at Tattershall (1430-50, fig. 47) and Ashby-de-la-Zouche (1474-83) in the fifteenth. It may be that the

really palatial edifices like Colchester, the Tower of London and Dover are not repeated later (*arx palatina*, William fitz Stephen called the White Tower in his twelfth-century description of London); but there is really no difference in principle between, say, Tattershall and Rochester, and their close relationship should not be obscured, as it has been before now, by calling the latter a tower keep and the former a tower-house – which, after all, are synonymous terms. The castle was basically a fortified residence, and the tower, perfectly combining defensive strength with residence and architectural symbolism, was a basic element in its design. 'You shall have the lordship in castle and in tower' (thus the envoys of Henry II's son, the young Henry, in 1173, seeking to win over the King of Scots to their rebellion by offering him the northern counties). The great tower as a donjon had all the lordly symbolism which the age required. It also had all the practicality demanded by its dual function, and lesser men were to take to tower residences, as strong-houses *par excellence*, in the pele towers of the north (figs. 100-1),

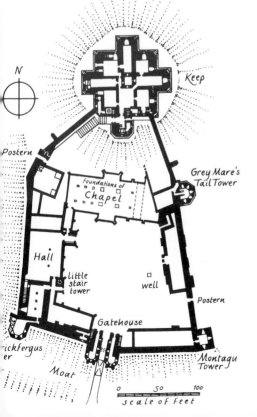

45 *At the turn of the fourteenth and fifteenth centuries, the third Percy lord of Warkworth, created earl of Northumberland in 1377, raised this remarkable great tower in place of an earlier keep upon the ancient motte of his castle of Warkworth. Ingeniously planned to contain the noble accommodation of a great lord, it is still partly residential and still crowns the ruins of the fortress. Cf. fig. 46.*

46 *Warkworth, Northumberland. The unusual keep of c. 1390 stands on the original motte.*

produced by the raids and counter-raids of the wars with Scotland in the later Middle Ages.

CURTAIN WALLS AND MURAL TOWERS

Whatever form the donjon of a castle took, it was, of course, only part of the whole, the inner sanctum of strength and lordship, and the whole had to be fortified and provided with additional secure accommodation. Stone walls – 'curtain walls' in castle terminology – soon generally replaced timber palisades, and in the further

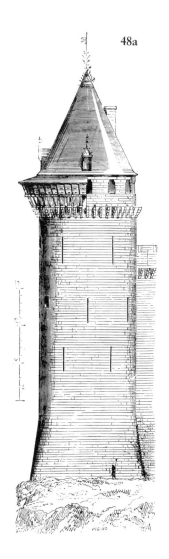

48a

47 *What principally remains of the castle of Tattershall in Lincolnshire built by Ralph lord Cromwell in the mid-fifteenth century is, appropriately, this great tower or donjon, machicolated at the head and containing the most noble accommodation.*

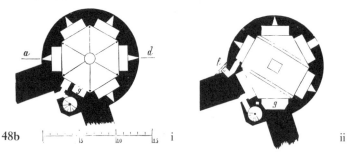

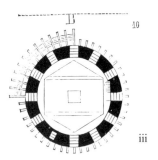

48b   i   ii   iii

48 *Mural tower for flanking fire. One of the great cylindrical angle-towers at Coucy-le-Château (Aisne), thirteenth century. (From Viollet-le-Duc,* Dictionnaire raisonné de l'architecture française, *article* Tour*). Elevation of north-west tower (a), plans of first, second and platform stages (b i-iii), cut-away drawing (c). Accommodation comprises a basement and three residential floors. Note the provision for lifting heavy goods. At Coucy the timber hoarding rested on stone corbels.*

54

strengthening of the enclosure no principle of medieval military architecture is more important than the use of projecting mural towers. Wall-walks and crenellation (battlements) helped, but it is difficult to defend the outer face and base of a long stretch of wall without leaning over and exposing oneself to the slings and arrows of outrageous fortune. Projecting galleries, timber hoarding or stone machicolation (see page 62), could be and were employed along the wall-head, but the best answer, because it incorporated yet other advantages, was the use of mural or flanking towers (fig. 48).

Such towers, by projecting from the outer face of the wall, enabled flanking fire (an inappropriate word before the use of fire-arms but unavoidable where 'shot', 'shoot' or

49 ABOVE *Timber hoarding in position on the inner and outer curtains of the city of Carcassone (Gard) and the rectangular flanking tower (Tour l'Evêque) which straddles them. (From Viollet-le-Duc,* Dictionnaire raisonné de l'architecture française, *article* Tour*).*

'shooting' may sound odd) to be directed upon it, and properly placed they thus enabled the whole *enceinte* to be covered by bowshot. At the same time, rising above the wallhead, they enabled that to be covered also should the enemy attempt to reach it by escalade, and they divided the wall, as it were, into sealed sections should it be breached at any point. The technique of the mural tower, of course, was inherited from the Roman past (e.g. Portchester, fig. 2) and was thus there, in castles no less than in towns and cities, from the beginning. There are references to timber towers incorporated in the palisades of early castles and archaeological evidence of them at the early motte-and-bailey site at Hen Domen (fig. 14). Le Plessis-Grimoult in Normandy incorporated stone towers in its curtain before 1047 (see page 27), and in England stone towers are set in the eleventh-century walls of Ludlow (fig. 18) and Richmond (fig. 17) castles. One of the earliest surviving examples of the complete and systematic use of mural towers survives at Henry II's Dover about his inner bailey (fig. 52) and also in that section of the outer curtain which is his to the north-east (fig. 51), and a complete set of very similar towers, open to the gorge or rear, studs the whole *enceinte* of the castle of Framlingham (fig. 53), built by Roger Bigod, earl of Norfolk, about 1190. All those so far listed have been rectangular in shape, except that both Dover (the Avranches Tower) and Framlingham used polygonal towers at awkward angles. The Bell Tower at the Tower of London, of late twelfth-century date, is polygonal at its lower levels and cylindrical above. Like the great tower, i.e. the tower keep, the mural tower usually becomes cylindrical (or 'D'-shaped) from the thirteenth century onwards, while the French fashion of the tower *en bec* appears at Dover (Norfolk and Fitzwilliam towers) early in Henry III's reign. Nevertheless Edward I deliberately chose polygonal towers for his castle at Caernarvon (fig. 85) for reasons of propaganda (the design evokes the Theodosian walls at Constantinople: see page 88), and rectangular towers may still be used in the later medieval centuries as they were, for example, at Pickering (fig. 43) and Rochester, or, indeed, in the quadrangular

50 *Machicolation (after Viollet-le-Duc,* Dictionnaire raisonne de l'architecture française, *article* Machicoulis).

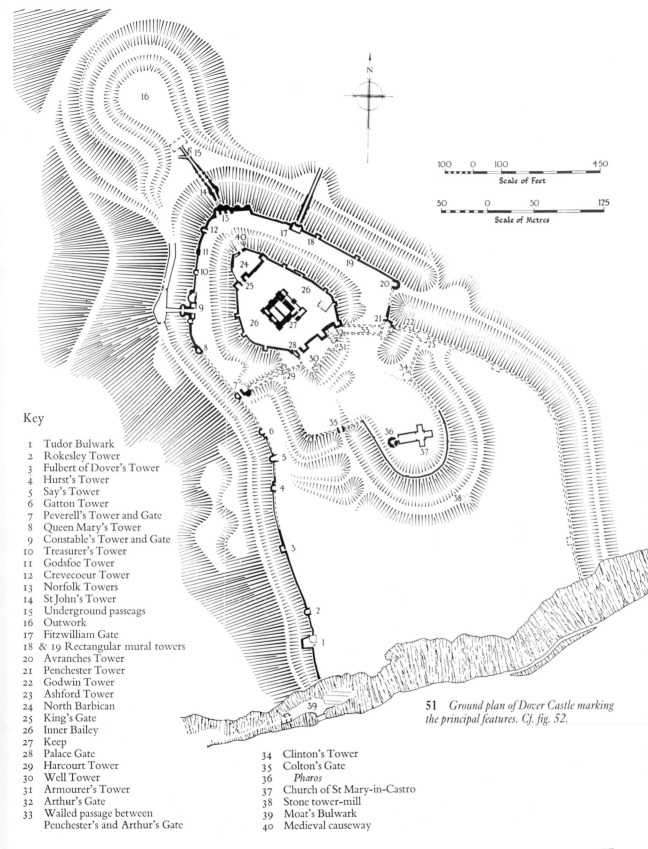

Key

1	Tudor Bulwark
2	Rokesley Tower
3	Fulbert of Dover's Tower
4	Hurst's Tower
5	Say's Tower
6	Gatton Tower
7	Peverell's Tower and Gate
8	Queen Mary's Tower
9	Constable's Tower and Gate
10	Treasurer's Tower
11	Godsfoe Tower
12	Crevecoeur Tower
13	Norfolk Towers
14	St John's Tower
15	Underground passeags
16	Outwork
17	Fitzwilliam Gate
18 & 19	Rectangular mural towers
20	Avranches Tower
21	Penchester Tower
22	Godwin Tower
23	Ashford Tower
24	North Barbican
25	King's Gate
26	Inner Bailey
27	Keep
28	Palace Gate
29	Harcourt Tower
30	Well Tower
31	Armourer's Tower
32	Arthur's Gate
33	Wailed passage between Penchester's and Arthur's Gate
34	Clinton's Tower
35	Colton's Gate
36	*Pharos*
37	Church of St Mary-in-Castro
38	Stone tower-mill
39	Moat's Bulwark
40	Medieval causeway

51 *Ground plan of Dover Castle marking the principal features. Cf. fig. 52.*

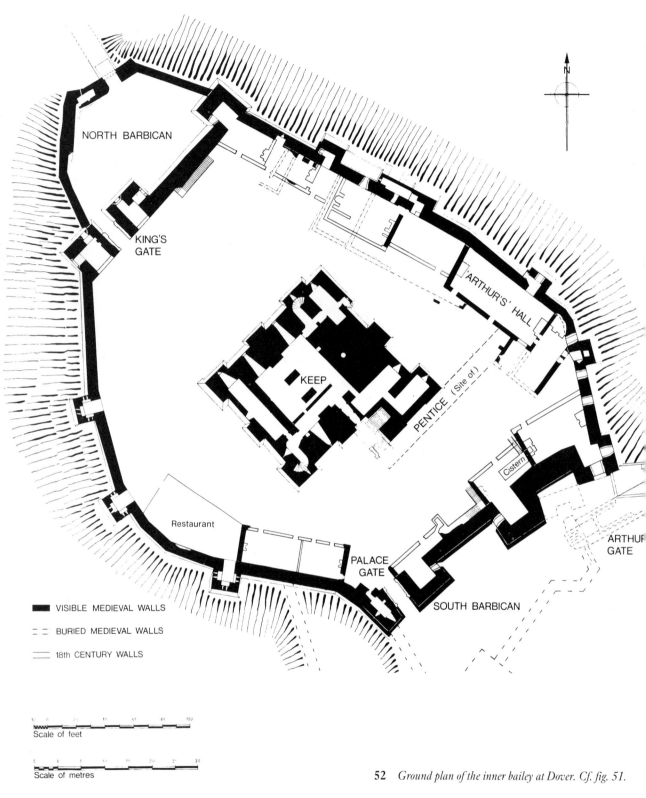

NORTH BARBICAN

KING'S
GATE

'ARTHUR'S' HALL

KEEP

PENTICE (Site of)

Cistern

Restaurant

PALACE
GATE

ARTHUR
GATE

SOUTH BARBICAN

■ VISIBLE MEDIEVAL WALLS

= = BURIED MEDIEVAL WALLS

— 18th CENTURY WALLS

Scale of feet

Scale of metres

52 *Ground plan of the inner bailey at Dover. Cf. fig. 51.*

castles of Middleham and Bolton-in-Wensleydale (figs. 68-9). Some of the great cylindrical and 'D'-shaped mural towers of the thirteenth century and later, Marten's Tower at Chepstow (figs. 54-5) above all, are almost on the scale of donjons in their majesty, and the way in which the drum-towers of Harlech (figs. 82-3) or Beaumaris (figs. 86-7), Conway (figs. 80-1) or Caerphilly (figs. 89-90), Rhuddlan (fig. 79) or Kidwelly (fig. 91), rise to bind their castles into a near-impregnable unit by the strength and raking range of bow-shot is impressive in the extreme. Immensely impressive also is the concentration of fire-power in these towered castles, or, to take individual instances, at the northern apex of Dover from the Norfolk Towers and their neighbours with the St John Tower thrust out in advance into the moat (fig. 51 and fig. 77), or the south front of Caernarvon where the arrow loops in the towers are joined and continued by the loops of galleries along the whole length of the walls between (figs. 84-6). And yet a century before this the ultimate exploitation of the principle of flanking fire is surely to be found about Richard I's inner bailey at Château-Gaillard (figs. 75-6)

53 *Framlingham in Suffolk, built in its present form in c. 1190, was a principal castle of the Bigod earls of Norfolk who were succeeded by the Mowbrays and the Howards. It is a good early example of the systematic use of mural towers. The obtrusive chimneys are Tudor.*

where individual towers are replaced by the curvilinear construction of the curtain wall itself in a continuous series of contiguous semi-circular projections. From that there could be no escape for any foe, nor was there meant to be.

GATETOWERS

From the beginning also, the entrance to the castle, a potential weak point, was given as much defensive strength as could be devised. There is probably here also a desire to impress and a certain symbolism attaching to the gateway of a noble's residence and reaching back into the Germanic past. Thus in England before the Conquest the compilation known as 'Of People's Ranks and Laws', written by Archbishop Wulfstan of York some time between 1002 and 1023, lists a gate (i.e. of some pretension) to his residence as one of the social qualifications a man needed to be raised to the rank of thegn ('fully five hides of land of his own, church, kitchen, a bell and *burgh-geat*, a seat and

59

54 *At Chepstow above the Wye in Monmouthshire there is something for everybody. A very early foundation soon after 1066 by William fitz Osbern, earl of Hereford, penetrating into Wales, the castle has one of the earliest stone keeps in the country (centre; later heightened). The lower bailey with the prodigious Marten's Tower (foreground), and the barbican or outwork (to the rear) were added at various dates in the thirteenth century. Cf. fig. 55.*

55 *Chepstow, Monmouthshire, ground plan. Cf. fig. 54.*

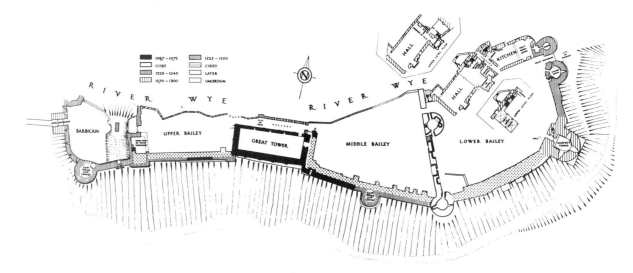

special office in the king's hall'), and we may be reminded of the description of the Carolingian royal residence or 'manse' at Annapes in Flanders about the year 800 with its 'gate of stone surmounted by a gallery'. An elaborate timber gatehouse was discovered in the excavations at Penmaen in Glamorganshire (which may not be a castle) dating from the twelfth century. In Normandy Le Plessis-Grimoult still shows a two-storeyed stone gatehouse which, like everything there, has to date from before 1047. Something very similar, its foundations now revealed by excavation, was evidently raised by the Conqueror at his new castle at Caen, built soon after 1047, and both evidently resemble the same Conqueror's gatehouse at Exeter (fig. 56), still standing more or less complete though later blocked and altered. The date of this is again early, going back to 1068 when the castle of Exeter was founded, and in type it is a strong tower of two storeys pierced by the entrance passage at ground level. The gateway, in short, is a gatetower, a mural tower of particular strength and elaboration.

This answer to the problem is very common in early castles, found, for example, originally at Ludlow and possibly Richmond (in both those cases the gateways were later converted into tower keeps) or at Castle Rising, and persists into the later Middle Ages at, for example, Framlingham, Leeds (Kent) and the so-called Bloody Tower at the Tower of London. A less impressive but evidently effective alternative was to have a perfectly straightforward gateway through the curtain wall but to cover it in the military sense by a strong mural tower built adjacent to it. This method of defending the entrance occurs quite frequently, and again is not exclusive to the early period, though it seems to be unnoticed by historians and 'castellologists' – thus it is, for example, at Montreuil-Bellay, and Clisson (both in France), at Melfi in Norman Italy, and even at the Tower of London where what later became the Bloody Tower began in the earlier thirteenth century as a mere gateway but defended by the great Wakefield Tower beside it (the two are integral in construction).

Nevertheless the great castle gatehouses

56 *Perhaps the earliest surviving castle gatehouse in England, this tower may well date from the foundation of Exeter castle by William the Conqueror in 1068. The entrance was through the lower and inner arch (now blocked) by a bridge.*

of the later Middle Ages which are such enormously impressive features of so many later castles are directly derived from the mural tower but incorporate in their structure not one but two. In England and Wales, in terms of surviving architectural remains, this type now begins at Henry II's Dover in the late twelfth century (figs. 52 and 57), where in the curtain of the inner bailey, dating from the 1180s, two of the rectangular mural towers are brought close together on either side of an entrance passage to make a strongly defended gateway – of which, in fact, there are two, the King's Gate and the Palace Gate, respectively north and south. (Like most of the towers at Dover

57 *At Dover in Kent the inner bailey and the keep within it (both here shown, cf. fig. 52) were the work of Henry II in the later twelfth century. The latter is one of the largest and finest rectangular tower keeps in the realm and contained the king's apartments. The curtain of the bailey systematically uses mural towers and the Palace Gate (centre right) consists of two such towers flanking the entrance.*

they were cut down to make gun-platforms and otherwise altered in the Napoleonic period, but are basically as designed by Henry II and his master mason.) The next stage, we may say, is the inner gate at Beeston, built about 1220, where the twin towers are cylindrical in the latest fashion and joined at the rear by their second storey over the entrance passage, thus forming a unified building, a gatehouse. From Beeston the way is straight, via the Middle and Byward Towers of Edward I's land-gate at the Tower of London, to the soaring majesty of Caerphilly (fig. 89) or Tonbridge (very similar gatehouses because the castles belonged to the same magnate, the Clare earl of Hertford and Gloucester, lord of Tonbridge and Glamorgan), Caernarvon (fig. 85) or Kidwelly (fig. 91), Harlech (fig.

82) or Beaumaris (fig. 86), or, in France and amongst many others, Villeneuve-lès-Avignon and Villeneuve-sur-Yonne (figs. 58-9). The prestige of the gatehouse was such that it remained an architectural feature of nobility or pretension even when the serious military strength of the castle had declined or vanished, as witness Herstmonceux (fig. 95) or Oxburgh Hall (fig. 96), Layer Marney or Hampton Court (fig. 97).

It is also at the gatehouse that we find, for obvious reasons, a concentration of many of the best-known defensive devices of medieval military architecture (fig. 60): a barbican (figs. 61-2) or outwork to the fore, perhaps, to keep an enemy at his distance (Portchester, Warwick, the Tower of London, Goodrich); a drawbridge (turning-bridge, *pont levis*, fig. 59 and fig. 106) crossing the moat or drawbridge-pit in front of the gate itself; hoarding or machicolation (e.g. Raglan) further to defend the approach (figs. 49 and 50 and fig. 92); the great iron-reinforced leaves of the gate reinforced again by a descending portcullis or iron grill (fig.

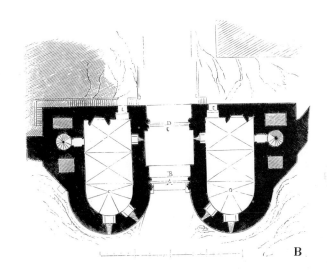

60); lateral arrow-slits defending the passage way, and murder-holes or *meurtrières* above, as much to quench any fire brought to the gate as to kill or harass assailants. Thus at the majestic King's Gate at Caernarvon (*c.* 1300), intended to be the state entrance to the castle from the town, albeit never completed, almost all these are used in multiplicity (fig. 85). There were to have been, first, a drawbridge across the northern ditch, and then no less than five great doors and six portcullises before another drawbridge. The passage way itself was intended to turn through a right angle and to be covered throughout by arrow slits and spy holes at various levels and no less than nine (perhaps more) *meurtrières* above. Abandon hope all ye who try to enter here! Caernarvon, after all, was built as the very centre of regality and royal government in newly conquered north Wales, and Edward I, with Eleanor his queen, might be housed in the state apartments in the Upper Ward. The result of all this was that in some of the fully developed castles of the later Middle Ages the gatehouse, a potential weak-point, became the strongest single building in the

58 *Gatehouse of the Fort St André at Villeneuve-lès-Avignon (Gard). (From Viollet-le-Duc,* Dictionnaire raisonné de l'architecture française, *article* Porte.) *Front elevation (A), ground plan (B) and cut-away drawing (C) of this magnificent mid-fourteenth-century gatehouse. The plan is basically of two towers, one on either side of the entrance passage, rising through two storeys, with a sort of command post placed centrally above the roof level. The whole is heavily machicolated and vaulted in stone throughout. The entrance passage itself is defended by two two-leafed doors and two portcullises with a* meurtrière *or murder-hole in front of the second.*

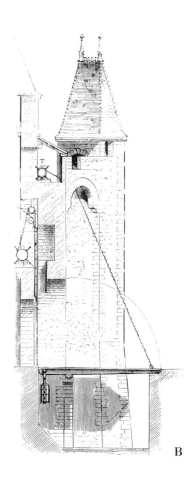

B

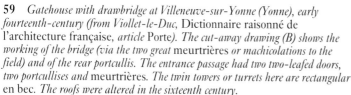

A

59 *Gatehouse with drawbridge at Villeneuve-sur-Yonne (Yonne), early fourteenth-century (from Viollet-le-Duc,* Dictionnaire raisonné de l'architecture française, *article* Porte*). The cut-away drawing (B) shows the working of the bridge (via the two great* meurtrières *or machicolations to the field) and of the rear portcullis. The entrance passage had two two-leafed doors, two portcullises and* meurtrières*. The twin towers or turrets here are rectangular en bec. The roofs were altered in the sixteenth century.*

60 OPPOSITE *Gatehouse – the Porte Narbonnaise at Carcassonne (Aude), late thirteenth-century (from Viollet-le-Duc,* Dictionnaire raisonné de l'architecture française, *article* Porte*). Front elevation (A), plans of first-floor (B1) and platform (B2) levels, cut-away drawing (C) and diagram showing working of second portcullis (D). Here the twin towers are en bec with spurs to the field, are stone-vaulted but have timber hoarding as opposed to stone machicolation about the head. The entrance passage is defended by a chain, two two-leafed doors, two portcullises, and murder-holes.*

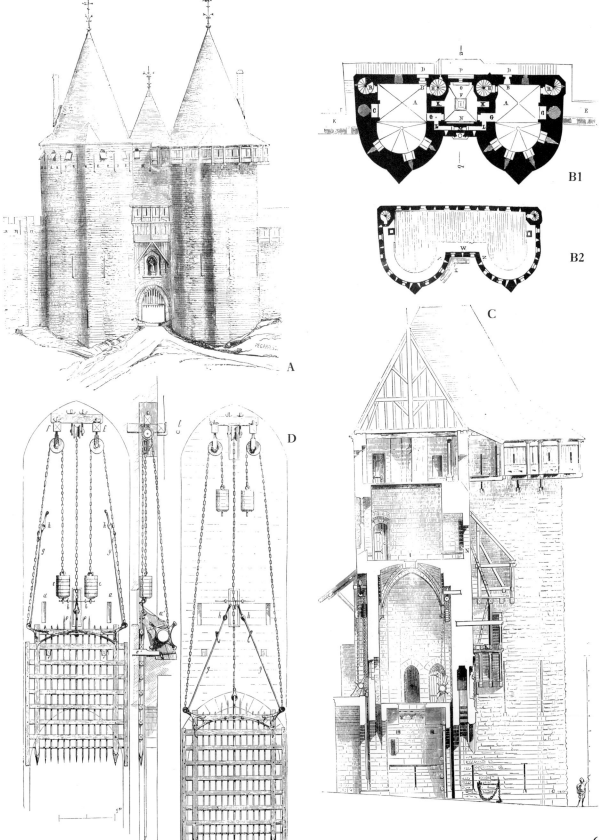

A

B1

B2

C

D

65

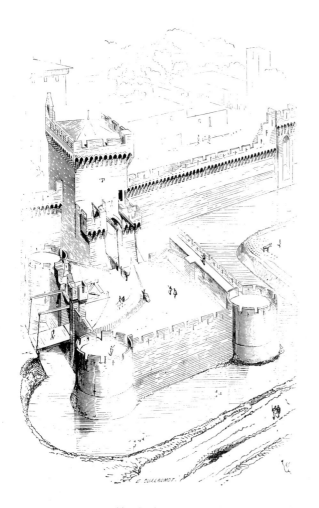

61 *Barbican or outwork before a gate. Reconstruction drawing of the Porte St-Lazare, c. 1368, at Avignon (from Viollet-le-Duc, Dictionnaire raisonné de l'architecture française, article Porte). Note the drawbridges and the machicolation of the gate, towers and ramparts of the city.*

whole castle, as it certainly was at Harlech or Beaumaris (at the latter there are two, fig. 87). The term 'keep gatehouse' has been coined in consequence by English archaeologists, and certainly the strength of the great gatehouse enabled it to contain some of the best residential accommodation. From the beginning to the end the castle was a lordly fortified residence, in purpose and function and no less in its several parts, and therefore the developed gatehouses and mural towers alike, while crucial to the defence, invariably contained chambers in their upper levels for the inmates. Never a

tower at the Tower of London, for example, without its comfortable accommodation, usually a residential unit of one or two chambers and a garderobe. There too, again as only an example, the grand chamber in the upper storey of St Thomas' Tower, *i.e.* the water-gate, looking over the Thames ('Sweet Thames run softly 'til I end my song') was intended for King Edward I himself who built it, while at Dover the splendid thirteenth-century Constable's Gate (figs. 63-4) has been from the beginning, and still is, the official residence of the Constable (now his Deputy).

OTHER RESIDENTIAL ACCOMMODATION

Nevertheless all this accommodation was not enough, even though we must add the donjon or keep containing the more private apartments of the lord and perhaps his closest and most honoured guest(s). Castles were extravagant and lordly. Though in practice for much of the time they might contain only a small permanent staff of constable, porter, watchmen or men-at-arms, they had to be able to provide the maximum accommodation that might be required, and to a suitable standard, as the peripatetic lord rode in with his household, his lady perhaps with her household, his guests with theirs, and all those attendant on them, and all their horses. Further, in an age of personal lordship and personal kingship, castles as residences of the great were the centres and headquarters of local government as well as estate management: they housed officials as well as lords and ladies. Hence a multiplicity of accommodation for a possible multitude of people, mostly of gentle birth.

There thus had to be certain communal buildings not yet specifically mentioned. A great hall will be required for state occasions, for no keep however palatial is likely to contain one large enough for that. Hence there was a great hall will at the Tower of

62 OPPOSITE *Lewes, Sussex. The fourteenth-century barbican or outwork shown here stands in front of the original, eleventh-century gatehouse as a fine piece of later-medieval fortification. The machicolation, the stone-built projecting parapet at the head, is to be noted. Cf. fig. 15.*

63 *The Constable's Gate at Dover castle was built in the 1220s to replace the former gateway at the northern apex of the castle damaged in the siege of 1216. In design like the Black Gate at Newcastle, its cluster of towers and forward thrust maximize the potential of flanking fire. Cf. fig. 64.*

London in the innermost bailey (shown, ruined, on the Haiward and Gascoigne plan of 1597, fig. 73), as well as the two halls, one on each floor, in the White Tower (fig. 20). Similarly, Conway had two halls, the great hall in the outer ward and the more private king's hall in the upper which is the donjon (fig. 81). There was also likely to be a communal kitchen, and also provision for communal worship in addition to the private devotions of chapels in keeps and oratories in chambers. Some castles housed ambitious religious foundations. Castle Acre Priory (Cluniac) and Stoke-by-Clare (Benedictine but with a difference as a daughter-house of Bec) are only two examples of monasteries at first founded close to their lord and patron in the bailey of his castle. St George's Chapel, Windsor (fig. 88), is the ultimate in England of the castle chapel, a collegiate foundation first established by Edward III to serve his chivalric Order of the Garter, also based on Windsor castle which in his reign was the Versailles of the age. Great halls, complete, restored or ruined, are to be seen in most castles. The eleventh-century Scolland's Hall at Richmond (fig. 17) is amongst the earliest in the kingdom although ruined; Oakham (fig. 65) survives magnificently from the twelfth century and Winchester

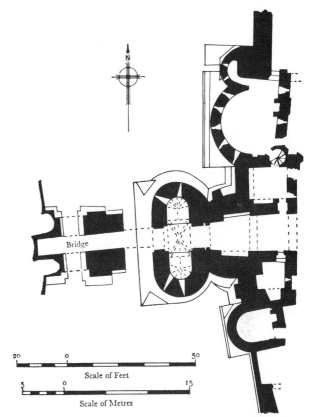

Bridge

Scale of Feet

Scale of Metres

64 *Plan of the complex Constable's Gate at Dover (c. 1221-7).*

65 *This splendid example of a late twelfth-century (c. 1180) stone-built aisled hall is all that remains upstanding within the earthworks of the bailey of Oakham castle in Rutlandshire.*

66 Kenilworth, founded by Geoffrey de Clinton in the earlier twelfth century, was developed into a splendid fortified palace by John of Gaunt in the fourteenth century, and again (with less regard for military strength) by the Elizabethan earl of Leicester in the sixteenth. In this view the tall windows of Gaunt's hall are on the left and Leicester's Building is on the right.

67 An aerial photograph of Warwick from the south shows the castle's whole architectural history from the motte (left, with trees) and bailey plan of the eleventh century to the splendid east front of Guy's Tower, gatehouse with barbican, and Caesar's Tower, built in the late fourteenth century. The much-developed main residential apartments stand safely above the river.

from the thirteenth; the ruined fourteenth-century hall of John of Gaunt at Kenilworth (fig. 66) still evokes the splendour of a royal prince. The episcopal kitchens at Durham, now serving University College and dressed in shiny tiles in the cause of modern hygiene, are still worth a visit, and so (if it can be gained) are Edward III's royal kitchens at royal Windsor, modernized (when last seen by the author many years ago) up to Queen Victoria's time, so that oxen could still be roasted, but by gas. In the development of these entirely residential buildings standing within the fortified walls of castles (and often in those parts least exposed to attack, fig. 67) there is little that calls for comment beyond the mere changes of architectural fashion. Each generation will produce the best and grandest that it can, for the context of castles is life at the top.

QUADRANGULAR CASTLES

We do, however, see something almost new in the quadrangular castles of the fourteenth and fifteenth centuries and later (the type shades off into the late medieval fortified manor houses like Oxburgh Hall or Herstmonceux – figs. 95-6). Here the

68 Bolton-in-Wensleydale is a quadrangular castle of the late fourteenth century, built by Richard, lord Scrope, in c. 1380. Like others of its kind, it was not designed to resist armies but was certainly a strong house, with suite after suite of lavish accommodation for the lord and his noble guests. Cf. fig. 69.

accommodation is arranged in neat, continuous and articulated fashion, two or three storeys high, about the four sides of a quadrangle which, with thick walls and turrets, arrow loops, gunports and crenellation, is in fact the castle. Bolton-in-Wensleydale (c.1380, figs. 68-9) and Bodiam (c.1385, figs. 70-1) are the classic surviving examples. Monastic buildings had, of course, been arranged in this way for centuries, and there are examples from at least the twelfth century of secular residences built on the quadrangular plan, even within castles as at Sherborne, Old Sarum, Henry II's royal lodgings in the upper bailey at Windsor, and John's elegant 'Gloriette' at Corfe. These, however, are separate residences planned independently of the castles in which they stand, just as elsewhere the various elements of residential accommodation, hall, chapel, kitchens and chamber-blocks, were disposed about the castle whose own plan is the result of military

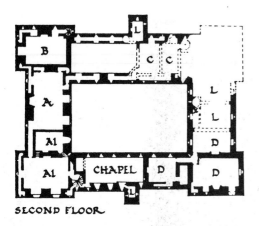

SECOND FLOOR

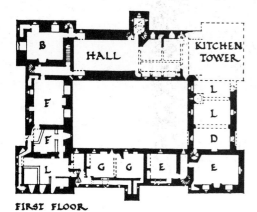

FIRST FLOOR

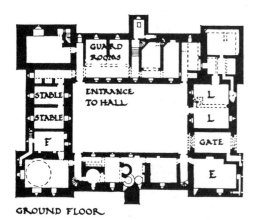

GROUND FLOOR

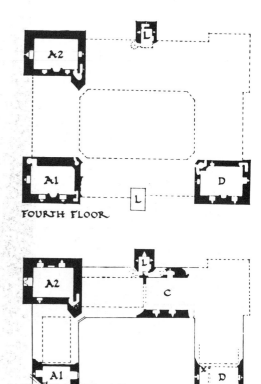

FOURTH FLOOR

THIRD FLOOR

APARTMENTS LETTERED A TO F
INDIVIDUAL LODGINGS ~ L

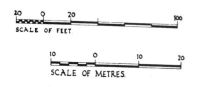

SCALE OF FEET.

SCALE OF METRES.

69 *Bolton-in-Wensleydale, Yorkshire. Floor plans showing accommodation (after Patrick Faulkner).*

70 OPPOSITE TOP *Bodiam in Sussex is the most photogenic of castles, standing in its wide water defences. Built c. 1385 by Sir Edward Dalyngrigge, it is quadrangular in plan with angle and intermediate towers, its gatehouse (right of centre) and postern (opposite at the rear) both machicolated. Cf. fig. 71.*

71 OPPOSITE BOTTOM *Bodiam, Sussex. Floor plans showing accommodation (after Patrick Faulkner).*

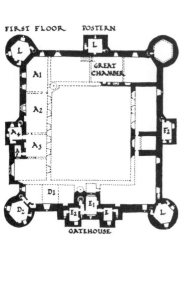

FIRST FLOOR   POSTERN

L
L
GREAT
CHAMBER
A1
A2
A4
A3
F2
D1
E1
D2
E2   L
L
GATEHOUSE

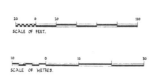

20   0   10   100
SCALE OF FEET.

10   0   30
SCALE OF METRES.

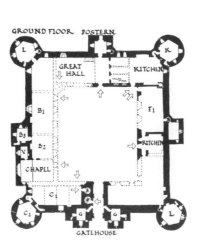

GROUND FLOOR   POSTERN

L
K
GREAT
HALL   KITCHEN
B1
F1
D3
D2   KITCHEN
V
CHAPEL
C1
C2   G   G   L
GATEHOUSE

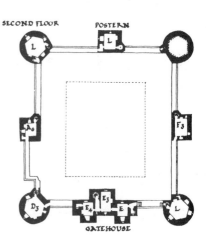

SECOND FLOOR   POSTERN

L
L
A6
F3
D3   E3
E4   E   L
GATEHOUSE

—N—

73

72 *Though much restored in the modern period, Leeds castle in Kent was developed into its present form and extent by Edward I for his queen, Eleanor, in the late thirteenth century. The castle's extensive water defences are its principal claim to fame and provide now the rare beauty of its setting.*

considerations and terrain, while everywhere chambers were inserted into towers and gates whose position is similarly determined. One might say, indeed, that the quadrangular castle of the later Middle Ages was the perfect form of castle architecture, the dual role of fortress and lordly residence blended in one integrated design, were it not for the fact that in all known examples, including Bodiam and Bolton, sheer military strength may be said to have given way a little to the domestic convenience of articulation.

ROCK AND WIDE WATER

Though Bodiam (fig. 70) is by no means among the strongest castles in the realm, it does show one technique of defence not so far noted, in its broad water defences whereby it stands in fact upon an artificial island. Many (though by no means all) castle moats, of course, had been water-filled for centuries, but wide sheets of water to keep an enemy even further at his distance is something else again and was, like siting one's castle on the living rock, one of the two best answers to undermining, the most devastating of all siege operations (see page 111). It may now be seen at its most impressive at the Clare castle of Caerphilly (fig. 89), or at Leeds castle, Kent (fig. 72 –

where the water lilies and the charm must not obscure the serious purpose), and formerly accounted for much of the strength of Kenilworth which in the mid-thirteenth century enabled it to hold out for six months against all the powers which the Lord Edward (son of King Henry III and the future King Edward I) could bring against it. English or Welsh castles sited upon rock are seldom so dramatically placed as some of those, for example, in Germany and the Rhineland, but yet are common where the terrain made it possible, as Conway (fig. 80) or Caernarvon (fig. 84), Harlech (fig. 82) or Goodrich show clearly enough. Yet again one must beware of attributing to progress and later development what we may only see by the chance of fortunate survival but was in fact present from the beginning. 'The Customs and Rights of the Duke of Normandy', drawn up in 1091, list castles built upon the rock or on an island as particularly requiring ducal permission.

5 Apogee and After

A book about castles obviously cannot describe, or even mention, every castle in the realm. Nevertheless, while everything that has been said so far about the development of the castle has been illustrated where possible by reference to particular features of particular castles, the best way next to bring it all together will be by describing certain castles which are outstanding by any standards and, more especially, show the best which any given period could produce. To choose the best may always seem invidious, but while the catalogue which follows could without doubt easily be extended, no one could deny the excellence of those castles it contains. One comment, however, must be made. Some of the finest castles in the land were built in one single

73 *A survey of the Tower of London made in 1597 by Haiward and Gascoigne shows the castle as it was finally developed in the later Middle Ages but with rot already setting in. Thus Edward I's landward entrance is all there but Ordnance Office stores and workshops disfigure the outer ward to the north and the palace buildings south of the White Tower are decayed.*

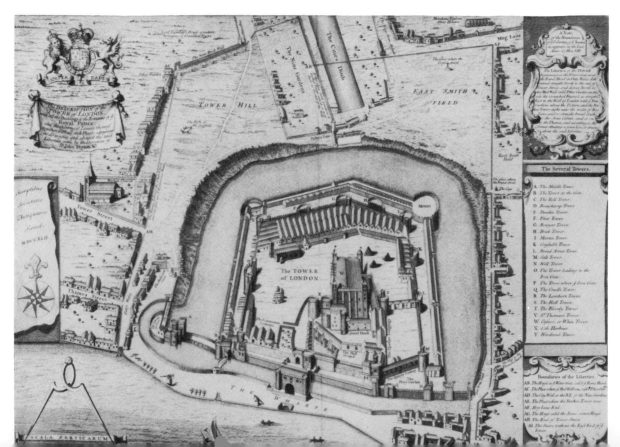

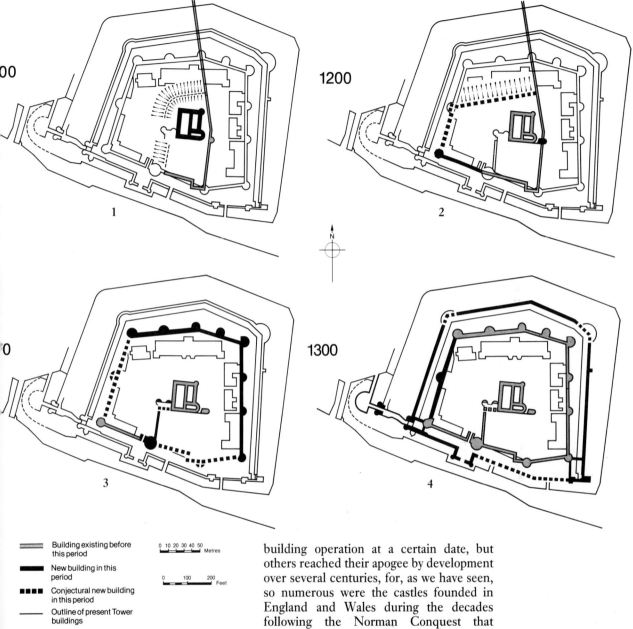

00

1200

1

2

0

1300

3

4

74 *The Tower of London, development plans at:*
1 c. *1100;*
2 c. *1200;*
3 c. *1270;*
4 c. *1300.*
*In each case earlier building is tinted and new building
shown solid. In 1 and 2 the pre-existing wall running
south and west is the Roman city wall.*

building operation at a certain date, but
others reached their apogee by development
over several centuries, for, as we have seen,
so numerous were the castles founded in
England and Wales during the decades
following the Norman Conquest that
thereafter new castles on new sites were
comparatively rare.

It may be coincidence but it also seems
significant that the finest specimen of
eleventh-century military architecture
surviving in the land is a great tower, namely
the Conqueror's White Tower at London
(figs. 9, 20-1, 74). This has been
sufficiently described previously (pages

75 *Château-Gaillard, built by Richard I on the border of Normandy above the Seine between 1196 and 1198, is one of the finest castles in Europe. The Butavant Tower is in the foreground; the unique inner bailey and keel-shaped donjon crown the whole position. Cf. fig. 76.*

31-2), and the point has already been made that the very similar tower at Colchester (fig. 22) from the same period was even more impressive when it was built. How sad it is then that both should now be disguised as museums, their purpose and their splendour within entirely hidden; the White Tower in particular, complete from top to bottom, stuffed to the brim with the no less splendid exhibits of the Tower Armouries. Such splendours cannot be combined with advantage but, rather, cancel each other out, and the White Tower, it must be stressed, as a wholly surviving royal and fortified residence of the second half of the eleventh century, now almost exactly eight hundred years old, is, or could be, unique in Europe, which in this context means the world (figs. 9 and 10).

Château-Gaillard

From the close of the twelfth century, a hundred years later, two castles at least can claim to be outstanding in combining all the techniques of fortification then known to such effect that they are not only amongst the finest castles of their period but of all succeeding generations also. Of Richard I's Château-Gaillard (the 'Saucy Castle') built on the chalk cliff above the Seine on the border of Normandy (figs. 75-6), in the amazingly short period of three seasons from 1196 to 1198, and at the then prodigious cost of some £11,500, all this and more may certainly be said. We must not leave it out of a book on English castles just because in some sense it is not English. Setting aside the fact that no castles in England, are, strictly speaking, 'English' in any case (still less 'Welsh'), but Norman and Anglo-Norman and thereafter, surely, Anglo-French (not for nothing has medieval England after 1066 been called a French colony), the Richard who built Château-Gaillard as duke of Normandy was also king of England, as well as count of Anjou and duke of Aquitaine. He was also the finest soldier of his age, when kings and princes were expected to be war leaders, and had only recently returned from his crusade to Jerusalem when building began. Into Château-Gaillard, therefore, went the experience of a lifetime's active campaigning and with no thought for expense.

The great castle thus already shows the principles of concentric fortification a century before such models of the type as

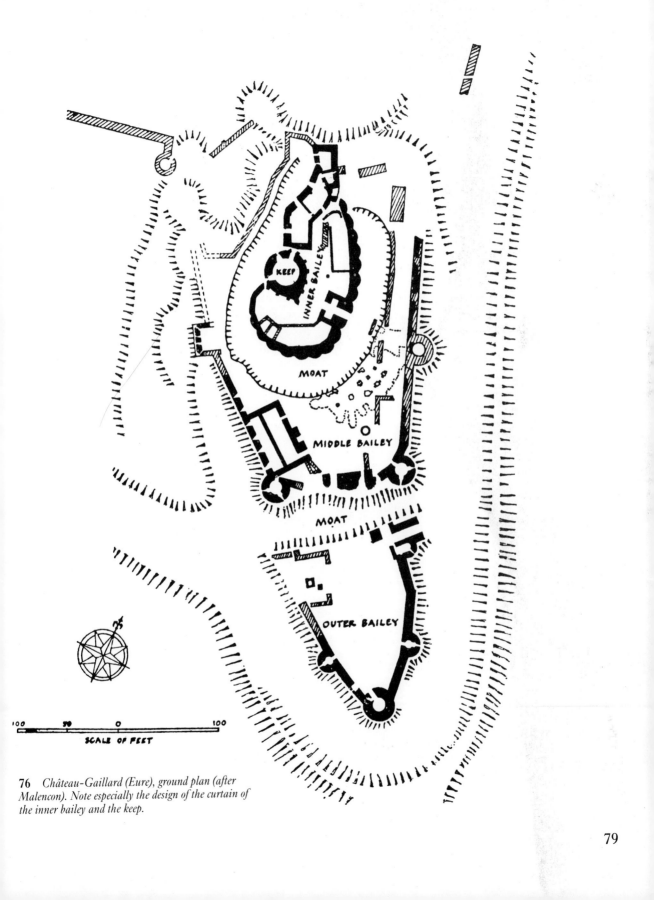

KEEP

INNER BAILEY

MOAT

MIDDLE BAILEY

MOAT

OUTER BAILEY

100   50   0   100

SCALE OF FEET

76 *Château-Gaillard (Eure), ground plan (after Malençon). Note especially the design of the curtain of the inner bailey and the keep.*

77 *Dover, Kent, from the north (1948). The Norfolk Towers, with the St John Tower out in front, are at the prow, the Constable's Gate on the outer curtain to the right, and Henry II's inner bailey and rectangular keep behind. The Anglo-Saxon church and Roman lighthouse are behind again. The first Norman castle was near the church. Cf. fig. 51.*

Beaumaris or Caerphilly, its tower keep (*en bec* and of almost unique design – see page 45) standing within an inner bailey which is itself more-or-less surrounded by the middle bailey. A dry ditch cut through the rock separates the inner and middle baileys and another cuts off the latter from an outer bailey thrust out to the scarped point of the promontory upon which the whole castle stands. At that point the great Butavant Tower stands like a mini-donjon, and this and most of the other flanking towers of the curtain wall are cylindrical in the latest fashion. The remarkable construction of the curtain of the inner bailey (page 59) provides what must be the ultimate in flanking fire as well as turning the force of any missile to a glancing blow, and into it the inner gateway is ingeniously set. All the defences are disposed, one after the other and interlocked, in the only direction from which attack can come, while the tailoring of the masonry to fit the living rock, and the scarping of the rock to fit the masonry, are of the utmost sophistication. Richard the Lionheart himself was so pleased with this his new castle at Les Andelys that he is said to have boasted that he could hold it even if its walls were made of butter, and it became a favourite residence of his last years, his letters and charters from it proudly dated *apud Bellum Castrum de Rupe* – 'at the Fair Castle of the Rock'.

Dover

Compared with Richard's Château-Gaillard, perhaps, Dover, built ten years before by his father Henry II, seems almost conservative if not old-fashioned, but was in fact the beginning of one of the finest castles in England (figs. 31-2, 51-2, 77). Here the work, concentrated in the decade 1180 to 1190, was a matter of development, more specifically the rebuilding and vast enlargement of a castle founded in 1066, intended to take in the whole area of the former Iron Age fortress and Old English borough upon the cliff top. The cost was great, some £7000, far exceeding any other known expenditure on any other royal building up to that time; yet even so the work was not completed by Henry's death, nor would it be for almost a century afterwards. Nevertheless, Henry II's contribution to the present Dover castle, 'the key of England' in Matthew Paris' thirteenth-century phrase, was very substantial, of high quality and advanced design, and most of it survives.

It principally comprised the great rectangular tower keep, the inner bailey about it, and a section of the outer curtain wall to north and east. The keep, perhaps the ultimate example of its type, has already been described (pages 43-4). The inner bailey is particularly distinguished by its systematic use of mural towers, rectangular and open to the gorge, less developed than those at Château-Gaillard a decade later but scarcely less effective. It is also distinguished by its gateways, of which there are two as a mark of confidence, one to the north (the King's Gate) and one to the south (the Palace Gate). Each had a barbican or outwork in front of it further to defend it, that to the north still surviving, while the design of the gateways themselves is especially worthy of note. Each, as we have seen (page 61), fundamentally consists of a pair of flanking towers brought in close together one on either side of the entrance passage, and they are thus, in terms of surviving examples, the precursors of all the greatest gatehouses of English castles in the later Middle Ages. How much of the outer curtain at Dover was completed by Henry II before his death in 1189 is uncertain, but his work certainly included the section on the north-east from a point just north of the Fitzwilliam Gate (a thirteenth-century insertion) to the Avranches Tower and thence southwards to the almost vanished Penchester Tower (and may have continued thence along the east to the cliff's edge, though all walling here has vanished). The surviving section is again strengthened by the characteristic rectangular and open-backed mural towers, and by the formidable sophistication of the polygonal Avranches Tower with its double tier of loops (plus vanished battlements), built to block the potentially dangerous re-entrant of the former Iron Age earthworks at this point. Lastly and not least important, the fact that Henry began the outer curtain in the 1180s means that again we find at Dover the principle of concentric fortification, a decade earlier than Château-Gaillard and a century before Edward I who is popularly supposed to have invented it.

EDWARDIAN CASTLES IN WALES

In the late thirteenth century, from 1277, Edward I embarked upon a castle-building programme which with good reason can only be compared with that which took place after the Norman Conquest of England. Edward's castle-works in Wales were an integral part of his conquest of Wales, and though the enterprise was smaller in scale than the hundreds of castles which mark the Norman Conquest, the size of the individual castles strengthened or constructed is infinitely larger than that of the castles of the eleventh century. In addition to the substantial strengthening and improvement of many existing castles in Wales and the marches of Wales, from Chester in the north to St Briavel's in the south, 14 new castles were built. Four – Hawarden, Denbigh, Holt and Chirk – were for the king's barons and marcher lords, and the remaining ten were royal, to be held by the king himself. Of the

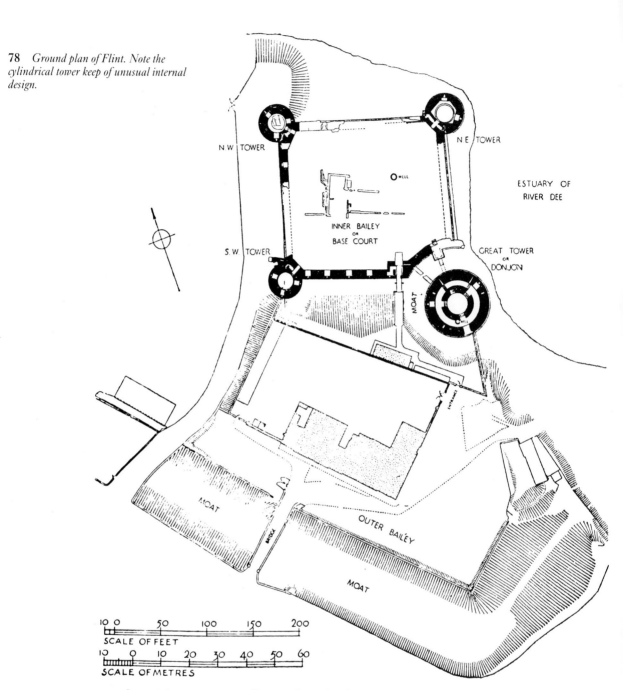

78 *Ground plan of Flint. Note the cylindrical tower keep of unusual internal design.*

N W TOWER

N E TOWER

ESTUARY OF
RIVER DEE

○ WELL

INNER BAILEY
OR
BASE COURT

S W TOWER

GREAT TOWER
OR
DONJON

MOAT

○ WELL

ENTRANCE

MOAT

BRIDGE

OUTER BAILEY

MOAT

10 0   50   100   150   200
SCALE OF FEET

10   0   10   20   30   40   50   60
SCALE OF METRES

latter, six were outstanding, and survive in large part – Flint and Rhuddlan, Conway and Caernarvon, Harlech and Beaumaris (figs. 78-87) – and all these were in the north, for North Wales, the principality of Gwynedd and the natural mountain fortress of Snowdonia, was then the heart of Welsh Wales and the principal centre of resistance.

The last-named four castles especially are simply amongst the finest anywhere in Europe, and it is important to stress the fact for reasons other than insular patriotism or local pride. They happen to have been built at a time when, arguably, the techniques of medieval military architecture attained their apogee; but it is not just a matter of technical progress and development. Edward I's castles in north Wales were built by a young

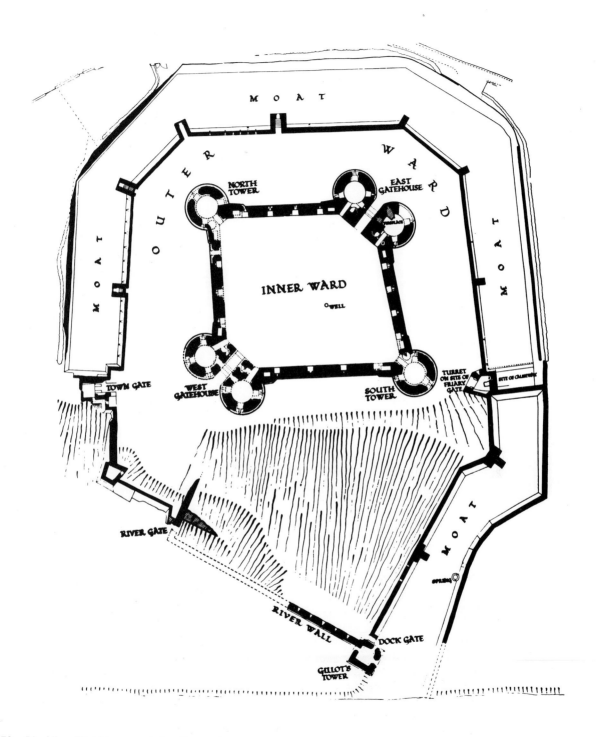

79 *Rhuddlan, Flintshire, ground plan. Concentric design with two gatehouses to the inner ward.*

80 *One of the four greatest Edwardian castles about Snowdonia, Conway was built with impressive speed between 1283 and 1287. Like Caernarvon it is tailored to the rock on which it stands, and is bound together into a defensible unit of prodigious strength by its series of (eight) mural towers. Cf. fig. 81.*

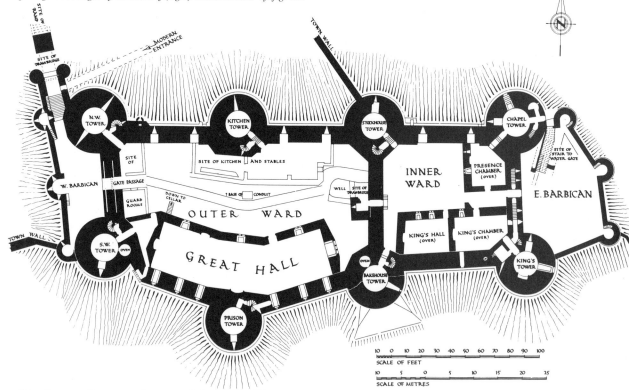

81 *Conway, Caernarvonshire, ground plan. Cf. fig. 79.*

82 *Harlech is amongst the finest of Edward I's castles in North Wales. Symmetrical and concentric, with four great drum towers at the angles and a huge twin-towered gatehouse to the east, its position was even stronger when tidal waters flowed in the valley at the foot of its rock. Cf. fig. 83.*

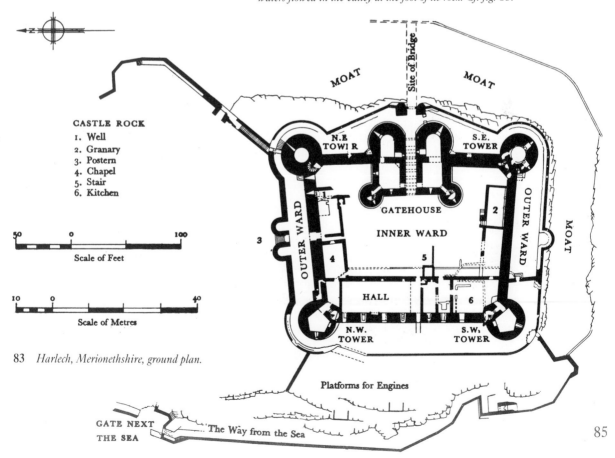

CASTLE ROCK

1. Well
2. Granary
3. Postern
4. Chapel
5. Stair
6. Kitchen

Scale of Feet

Scale of Metres

83 *Harlech, Merionethshire, ground plan.*

84　*Deliberately the most impressive of all Edward I's new castles in North Wales as the centre of royal government in the conquered principality, Caernarvon invokes imperial claims by its site in Roman Segontium and its polygonal towers and banded masonry copied from the Theodosian wall at Constantinople. Cf. fig. 85.*

king in his pride; as part of the extension of his kingdom in accordance with new (and old) imperial notions; by a king, moreover, who (like Richard I) was an outstanding warrior – the finest lance in Europe, men said of Edward 'Longshanks', whose long legs gave him a firm seat in the saddle; and, lastly, were built almost regardless of expense by a king who was amongst the richest and most powerful princes in all Latin Christendom – though money and its shortage will come in before the end, and Caernarvon and Beaumaris have never yet been finished to this day. They were built, too, not only by King Edward, who helped to plan them and financed them, but by one who is surely amongst the greatest architects in English history, Master James of St. George, master-mason and engineer, whom the king had recruited from Savoy (now part of Switzerland) where his cousin was the prince. Finally, it is to be noted that six of Edward's Welsh castles – Denbigh, Aberystwyth, Flint, Rhuddlan, Caernarvon

and Conway – were planned and built from the beginning in association with their respective fortified town, and that all six of the major royal castles in the north were built with direct access to tidal waters (in the case of Rhuddlan the whole course of the river Clwyd was altered along an artificial channel between two and three miles long to make this possible) so that they could both be reinforced by sea and play their part in the kind of joint campaigns by sea and land which conquered Wales.

Caernarvon

Of all of these castles we will take Caernarvon (figs. 84-5) first. Amongst the last to be begun – with Conway and Harlech in the spring of 1283 – it was intended from the beginning to be the finest, the centre and seat of royal government in the north, and the especial symbol of the king's new lordship. A glance at a ground-plan of the castle (fig. 85) shows at once its overall design and form – a narrow-waisted enclosure whose shape is determined by the rock on which it stands and also, though to a lesser extent, by the motte of a much earlier castle of the eleventh century deliberately retained and incorporated in the inner or upper bailey to the east. The whole is bound together into one integrated and eminently defensible unit

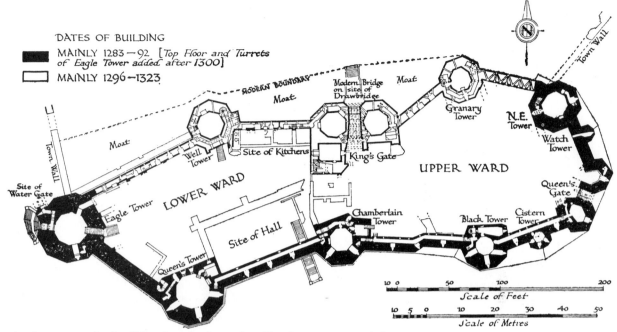

DATES OF BUILDING

■ MAINLY 1283—92 [*Top Floor and Turrets of Eagle Tower added after 1300*]

□ MAINLY 1296—1323

Town Wall

MODERN BOUNDARY

Moat

Moat

Modern Bridge on site of Drawbridge

Moat

Granary Tower

N.E. Tower

Watch Tower

Town Wall

Moat

Well Tower

Site of Kitchens

King's Gate

UPPER WARD

Queen's Gate

Site of Water Gate

Town Wall

Eagle Tower

LOWER WARD

Site of Hall

Chamberlain Tower

Black Tower

Cistern Tower

Queen's Tower

10 0   50   100   200
Scale of Feet

10 5 0   10   20   30   40   50
Scale of Metres

by the great and splendid series of polygonal mural towers, so disposed about the whole circumference as to lay flanking fire upon all of it, and reinforced along the south front by two firing galleries, one above the other in the thickness of the wall (intended also on the north front but never provided). All this combined with the crenellated summits of the walls and towers must have provided one of the most formidable concentrations of fire-power to be found in the Middle Ages. The most majestic of the mural towers is the Eagle Tower at the west end, singled out by the further distinction of its three turrets, each of which originally had a stone eagle upon it. This tower was almost the donjon of the castle and contained some of the best residential accommodation, rising three storeys above the water-gate and entrance vestibule in its basement.

The whole castle, of course, was replete with ample and sumptuous accommodation, fit to house not only the resident constable and 'justiciar' of Wales with his own household, but also the king himself, his queen, the prince of Wales, each with their own households should they come. As at Conway, the inner sanctum to contain the apartments of the king and queen, which were never completed, was intended to be in

85 *Caernarvon, ground plan.*

the inner or upper bailey, to be cut off from the outer or lower bailey by fortified buildings, never completed either, running from the King's Gate to the Chamberlain Tower. In addition to the water-gate in the Eagle Tower already mentioned, there were two main land-gates to the castle, each on the now almost standard plan of two flanking towers one on each side of the entrance passage. The King's Gate on the north front was the state entrance from the walled and fortified town of Caernarvon, built at the same time as the castle, and its manifold defences have already been described (page 63). The Queen's Gate, still unfinished, led into the inner and royal bailey and was approached from outside by a lofty ramp and drawbridge, the great height of the actual entrance and its towering arch being dictated by the ancient and symbolic motte retained within (now gone). By the end of Edward's reign in 1307 some £27,000 had been spent on Caernarvon castle, though the work was not complete, i.e. twice as much as the total cost of Conway (£14,000 between 1283 and 1287), and three times the cost of Henry II's Dover or Richard's Château-Gaillard.

Further, there was more to Caernarvon

than immediately meets the eye, for the royal fortress was amongst other things a conscious architectural exercise in symbolism and propaganda. The careful but inconvenient retention in the upper bailey of the motte of the former castle of Earl Hugh of Chester, dating back to the first Norman penetration of North Wales in the late eleventh century, was meant to emphasize that King Edward's campaigns in Wales were no new conquest but the reassertion of ancient right now vindicated. And there were also more elevated claims than this made manifest by the new castle. In this period of the formation of national monarchies in France and England, imperial ideas derived from Roman Law were current. In France the lawyers of Edward's rival, Philip the Fair, proclaimed that 'the king of France is emperor in his kingdom', and in England also the law-giving king had notions of imperial hegemony over all Britain. It was no accident that the site selected for the principal castle in north Wales and the seat of intended royal government was the former Roman city of Segontium, with its legendary imperial past. In 1283, the very year of the castle's foundation, what was believed to be the body of the Emperor Magnus Maximus (383-8), allegedly 'father of the noble Constantine' himself, had been found there and reburied in the church by the king's command. Moreover, there was current in Wales at this time, and presumably known to Edward, the romance of Maxen Wledig, i.e. of Magnus Maximus (still preserved for us in the Welsh *Mabinogion*), which told how, long ago, that same emperor had dreamt of journeying from Rome to a land of high mountains, and of coming to a river flowing into the sea, and of seeing opposite the land an island; of how in his dream he had seen a great fortified city at the mouth of the river, and a great fort in the city, the fairest that man ever saw, and great towers of many colours on the fortress, and in its hall a chair of ivory with the image of two eagles in gold thereon. 'To all this the castle which Edward . . . began to build at the mouth of the river Seiont and opposite the island of Anglesey was plainly intended to give substance, to be both the fulfilment of the tradition and the interpretation of the dream' (A.J. Taylor in *The History of the King's Works*, ed. H.M. Colvin [HMSO, 1963], p. 370).

This, then, is why Caernarvon castle looks to this day different from the other castles of Edward I in Wales, its polygonal towers and banded masonry a deliberate evocation of the Theodosian wall at Constantinople, the Emperor Constantine's own city, and hence the Eagle Tower, and hence the eagles in stone thereon. There is something immensely impressive, still after 700 years, in the concentration of effort and will which Edward brought to bear upon his wars in Wales, and the focusing of so much resource, not only skill and men and money, but also history, legend and romance, upon Caernarvon in particular. All this is medieval personal monarchy in action, and with all this in mind one cannot suppose it was mere accident that brought Eleanor, his queen, to Caernarvon to bear their first-born son in April, 1284 – the future Edward II but also Edward 'of Caernarvon' and the first English Prince of Wales.

Beaumaris

Only by the near-unique standards of Caernarvon, intended from the first to be the showplace of Wales and the principal strength and symbol of the new régime in the principality, were the other major new castles built by Edward I about Snowdonia – Conway, Harlech and Beaumaris – any less impressive. Harlech (figs. 82-3), on its towering rock, was built and completed at a total cost of some £9500 between 1283 and 1290; Conway (figs. 80-1) with prodigious speed between 1283 and 1287 at a cost of £14,000. Beaumaris (figs. 86-7), begun on the Isle of Anglesey in the third Welsh war of 1294-5, was, after an expenditure of well over £14,000, like Caernarvon never completed, but it must serve as our second example of the perfect late-thirteenth century castle because it is built on the concentric plan which Edward I is often erroneously said to have invented. That plan, followed with a classic precision, was here adopted because the site, unlike the site of Harlech or Conway or Caernarvon, each set upon the rock, has no natural advantages. The castle was set in flat, low-lying, marshy ground, and in consequence its defences were doubled, one line within another. Of

86 *Beaumaris on the Isle of Anglesey was the last of Edward I's great castles in North Wales (1295- c. 1330) and was never finished. On flat land, it is a perfect example of concentric design, one enclosure within another and the whole surrounded by a wide, water-filled moat. Cf. fig. 87.*

these, of course the inner *enceinte*, the castle proper, is by far the stronger and rises well above the outer which serves as an advanced screen. The whole is surrounded by a broad, water-filled moat (like Edward's Tower of London, developed by him into another great concentric castle as we see it now), and the outer curtain is liberally supplied with loops (for crossbows) and cylindrical projecting mural towers of which the largest stand at the four main angles. The main, inner, enclosure has curtain walls nowhere less than 16ft thick, four bold drum towers at the four angles, two 'D'-shaped towers projecting even further in the centre of the east and west sides, and not one but two thundering great gatehouses, each of the twin-towered plan, respectively north and south.

Of course as a castle fit for a king, Beaumaris was intended to contain more than ample residential accommodation of the highest quality: there were to be five main suites in all, two, one above the other, in each of the gatehouses and another, comprising great hall and a range of chambers in association with the Chapel Tower, along the

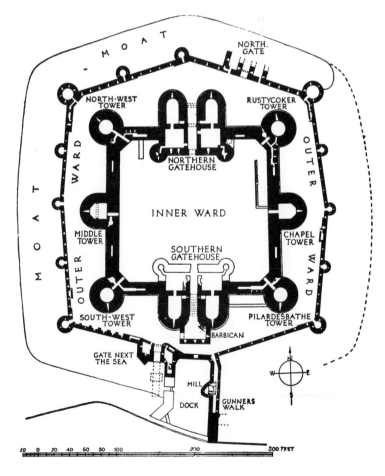

87 *Beaumaris, Anglesey, ground plan.*

east side of the inner ward but never built. There was a dock for sea-going vessels attached to the castle on the south, by the 'Gate next the Sea', further sheltered by its own spur wall (Gunners Walk) and the intended wall of the borough which also was never built. As Beaumaris stands (and as it has stood incomplete since the fourteenth century) none of the great flanking towers of the inner curtain save that at the north-west angle rises to its full height, nor does either of the gatehouses, while the rear half of the southern gatehouse has not been built above the foundations, but there is more than enough to show the scale and majesty of its conception by King Edward and Master James of St George, master of the king's works in Wales.

WINDSOR AND THE TOWER OF LONDON

It is very tempting to continue the piecemeal description of the finest castles in the land. At least we must mention two, Windsor (fig. 88) and the Tower of London (figs. 73-4), as examples of castles not raised in one single operation like Richard I's Château-Gaillard or Edward I's new castles in north Wales, but developed continuously after 1066 to reach their ultimate and present form in the thirteenth and fourteenth centuries. Both became virtual fortified palaces, as Windsor still is, and the monarchs especially responsible for their final development were Henry III and Edward I at the Tower and Edward III at Windsor. The scale of the works involved, as well as the splendour of the results, becomes apparent when it is realized that, although undertaken at what were already major castles before they began, Edward I's works alone at the Tower of London cost some £21,000 between 1275 and 1285, and Edward III's at Windsor between 1350 and 1377 cost no less than £51,000 – the highest recorded figure for any

88 *Windsor castle from the air. A royal castle from the Conquest to now, Windsor began as a motte-and-bailey (with two baileys) and has acquired stone buildings in almost every reign from William the Conqueror to William IV. Edward III made of it the fortified palace it has ever since remained. The fifteenth-century St George's Chapel is central in the lower bailey.*

single building operation in the whole history of the kings' works in the Middle Ages. It must also be pointed out that the fact that all the castles so far described in this section have been royal does not mean that all the best castles were the king's. Other great lords, the king's barons, and some bishops also, had castles too, and we shall not understand feudal society if we do not recognize that there is no necessary architectural distinction, in strength or splendour, between royal and non-royal castles – nor, for that matter, shall we understand it if we suppose that baronial castles, or barons themselves, were somehow inimical to the king's majesty, The king had more castles than any other lord because of his function as the greatest lord of all, the lord of lords and feudal suzerain, but very many castles, including some of the finest in his realm, were held of him by his vassals and his magnates. Two examples only must illustrate the point.

Caerphilly

Caerphilly (figs. 89-90) in Glamorgan in south Wales certainly makes the point, for it has been called 'the greatest of the Welsh castles', and may be thought in some respects to exceed in strength and excellence even the finest of King Edward's castles in the north, which indeed it antedates at least in conception. And this befits its lords who were the greatest magnates in the land – the Clare earls of Hertford and Gloucester, lords of Glamorgan, of Tonbridge in Kent and of Clare in Suffolk (hence the name). It is known that the castle at Caerphilly was begun in 1271 as a second attempt (the first, in 1268 on a site probably a little to the north-west, having been destroyed by the Welsh prince Llewelyn ap Gruffyd), but thereafter the loss of all building accounts and the absence of any other documentation prevent our knowing the sequence of the work, or its cost, or the time taken to complete it – though completed it certainly was, unlike either Caernarvon or Beaumaris. The outcome, however, beggars all description.

The castle proper is a concentric fortress fully worthy to be compared with Beaumaris. The outer ward, revetted by the low, crenellated outer curtain, forms a surrounding platform which, being itself

89 *Though now surrounded by unlovely urban sprawl, Caerphilly in Glamorgan can claim to be the finest castle in all Wales and England. It was built in the late thirteenth century by the Clare lord of Glamorgan, earl of Hertford and Gloucester, on the concentric plan, with wide water defences controlled by the screen wall of fortified sluices in the foreground. Cf. fig. 90.*

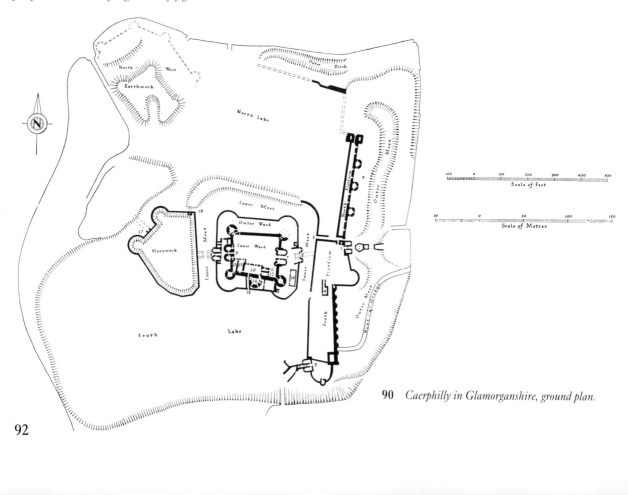

90 *Caerphilly in Glamorganshire, ground plan.*

shaped to provide flanking fire, has and needs no towers save for its two twin-towered gateways east and west. It has in addition a water-gate to the south, covered by the huge Kitchen Tower behind it, and there may have been another water-gate to the north. The inner ward, entirely commanding this outer platform, is the main strength of the castle. It is an irregular rectangular enclosure, bound together by the four cylindrical angle towers, each designed as a separately defensible unit, the massive Kitchen Tower in the centre of the south front, and two vast twin-towered gatehouses east and west, the former the larger of the two. The great hall (slightly later than the main fabric and much restored) and the rest of the principal residential accommodation line the south side of the court, and there are, of course, other residential suites in the towers and gatehouses. In addition to all this, Caerphilly has the sweeping feature of its Eastern Front, a long screen of curtain walls and platforms strengthened by projecting towers and buttresses, the magnificent series of flanking buttresses along its southern end being comparable in its sophisticated effect only to the inner curtain of Richard I's Château-Gaillard (fig. 76). The purpose of this immensely formidable outer defence, thrust forward and pierced by the outer gate, is to bar the main approach from the east and also to dam and control the waters of the marsh in which the castle stands, thus to form the great lakes which entirely surround the inner fortress and give Caerphilly the most elaborate water defences in all Britain. Finally, and in addition to all this again, there was the Hornwork, barring the western approach, an outwork consisting of a scarped and stone-revetted island, its entrance from the west by a drawbridge guarded by two boldly projecting bastions, and connected with the main castle by another drawbridge leading to the western outer gate.

Kidwelly

Caerphilly was an entirely new castle on a new site when it was first built in the late thirteenth century. Kidwelly, (fig. 91), of comparable date (begun c.1275) represents the entire rebuilding on the same site of an earlier, twelfth-century castle, planted there with its attendant fortified town by Roger,

Bishop of Salisbury, in the time of Henry I. The work was begun by Payn de Chaworth and completed by Henry of Lancaster (nephew of Edward I) who married the Chaworth heiress in 1298. The result, we may say, is a concentric castle with a difference. The quadrangular inner ward (cf. Caerphilly, Harlech and Beaumaris) is defended by four great, boldly projecting drum towers at the four angles. It is further and sufficiently defended on the east by a steep drop to the river, but on its other three sides is defended by the arc of the Outer Ward whose towered curtain, with two twin-towered gatehouses (north and south), follows the line of the earthworks of the original castle. The main and grand residential apartments on the east side of the inner sanctum of the Inner Ward – hall, solar, kitchens, and a splendid chapel projecting out eastward on a spurred base towards the river – probably date to c.1300 and the outer curtain to the early fourteenth century. The most impressive single feature of the castle, the great southern gatehouse (with its machicolation) is the result of a substantial reconstruction between 1399 and 1422.

DECLINE

If, next, after these splendid examples of the castle in England and Wales at its apogee, we turn to its decline, we must do so with some caution in a number of respects. First, we simply do not know as much as we should about the castle in the later medieval period, historians or, rather, archaeologists (since historians in the main have concerned themselves little with the whole subject), having concentrated chiefly on the period of origins, early development and ultimate achievement. Second, castles, like feudalism of which they are the product, show a marked reluctance to be hustled off the stage by historians ever anxious to proclaim change. In the light of recent research the so-called 'Bastard Feudalism' of the later Middle Ages looks increasingly like the real thing, just as the so-called 'tower houses' of e.g. Tattershall (fig. 47) or Ashby-de-la-Zouche look or at least function much like the tower keeps of old. New castles may still be raised as necessary, like the fifteenth-century

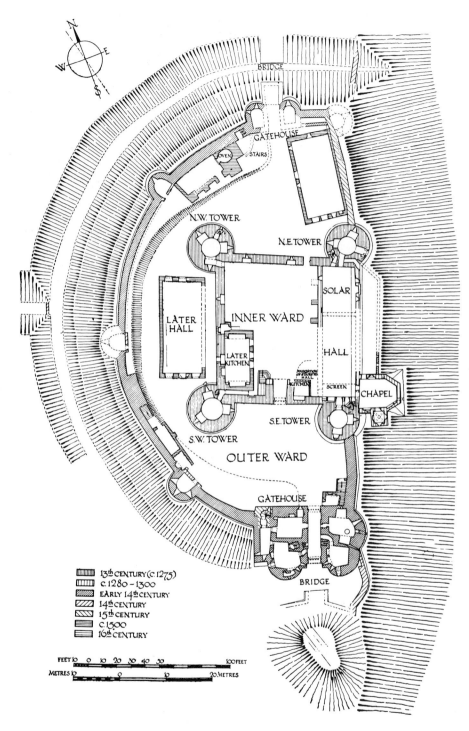

91 *Ground plan of Kidwelly, Carmarthenshire – a concentric castle with a difference.*

Raglan (technically a rebuilding, but complete, fig. 92), which shows no noticeable lowering of the guard and even has a great tower, i.e. the hexagonal Yellow Tower of Gwent, standing upon the ancient motte. New works of entirely serious fortification could be added to existing castles as they certainly were at Warwick (fig. 67) in the late fourteenth century, in the new east front towards the town, with its elaborately defended gatehouse and barbican in the centre and the great Caesar's Tower and Guy's Tower respectively at either end. If the prodigious sums spent by Edward III upon Windsor in the second half of the fourteenth century were almost wholly devoted to its residential splendour, it is to be remembered that castles in all periods contained the most splendid accommodation that the age could produce and the lord afford, and it would be difficult to show that the defences of Windsor were in any way weakened by this development. If, as we are

92 *Raglan in Monmouthshire is a late medieval (fifteenth-century) castle which never showed any sign of weakness. It was accordingly viciously 'slighted' by Parliament after its triumphant resistance for Charles I. Shown here are the machicolated gate towers and (off, left) the free-standing donjon, the 'Yellow Tower of Gwent'.*

sometimes told, the military importance of the castle declined in the later Middle Ages, some castles at least show little awareness of the change, and it is always salutary to remember that many played an important role, and held out nobly, in the seventeenth-century Civil War (which, though 'Civil War' to us, Clarendon called the 'Great Rebellion', which is in turn a feudal and a medieval notion).

Nevertheless, what happens in the end – in England, let us say, in the sixteenth century – is that the duality which had made a castle is divorced, and the unique combination of lordly residence and fortress falls asunder. The new residences of the great like Hampton Court (fig. 97) or Nonesuch are no longer seriously fortified

93 *Deal, Kent, was the largest of the Tudor forts (cf. Sandown, Walmer) built in 1539-40 to defend the anchorage of the Downs. Like the others a mere emplacement for heavy guns and exclusively military, it is no castle though usually called one.*

(though, of course, there had been unfortified palaces, manors and hunting lodges in the medieval period), and the new fortresses – Deal (fig. 93), Walmer, Camber, St Mawes and the rest – are in no real sense residences but purely military. They are also, it is to be noted, exclusively royal; and this, it may well be, provides the best clue to an answer to the question Why? In the waning of the castle in its true dual function of residence and fortress we are witnessing a change in the whole nature of society, and therefore, with it, the state. All architecture, it has to be admitted, faithfully reflects – is, indeed, the product of – the society which creates it, its needs and aspirations as well as its technical abilities. At the beginning of this book it was shown how the castle was the particular manifestation of feudal society, and now with the castle's decline we have to recognize that society's approaching end. Fashion, of course, has something to do with it. The Renaissance prince prefers Whitehall. But, more profoundly, we are taught that one of the characteristics of feudalism is the fragmentation or decentralizing of political power, and with it the devolution of much military power also.

All this castles may be said to represent and symbolize, for whatever control the king or prince as feudal suzerain may have retained over fortifications, there were always more which we can only call baronial than those which were directly royal. Feudalism, we are also taught, is society organized for war. It is not unique in that respect (cf. Britain in 1940), but it is unique in the methods it employed; and in recognizing its controversial beginnings and no less controversial ends we shall not go far wrong if we follow a pattern in European history wherein fortification and military power, once the exclusive attribute of the Roman and sovereign state, is diffused in the ninth and tenth centuries to great lords on the spot, and not finally gathered together again in the hands of a central authority until the development of sixteenth-century national monarchies and Machiavelli's prince.

Even so, let no one suppose that in English history anything significant happened in 1485, though still proclaimed in old-fashioned books which still abound as the year of the advent alike of Tudor 'New Monarchy' and the 'modern' period. Nor can it any longer be maintained that the advent of gunpowder, for long the most popular and portmanteau reason adduced for the decline of the castle, had anything directly to do with it. For one thing, gunpowder was probably first used in warfare in this country in the late thirteenth century (at the siege of Stirling by Edward I in 1297?), at the very time when some of the finest castles in the realm were being built, as others were maintained, improved and built and used long after. Not for another two centuries and more do we find medieval military architecture rendered obsolete by Hotspur's 'foul stinking bombards', and a new type of fortress, like the Tudor coastal forts of Henry VIII (fig. 93) and his successors, built on new principles of fortification to resist and also to mount the heavier cannon that had been developed. Until then the only obvious effect of the new guns, used as much in defence as attack, upon castle architecture is the appearance of gunports through which they could be trained and sighted. Had the sixteenth-century nobility, still holding to the traditions of a military aristocracy albeit for

94 *Wingfield, Suffolk, was a castle of moderate strength built by Michael de la Pole, earl of Suffolk, in c. 1384. Of local flint with decorative flushwork, it was fashionably quadrangular in plan, with angle towers and an impressive gatehouse. The mid-sixteenth-century timber-framed house shown here is a late conversion after the great days were over.*

the most part *parvenu*, required or been allowed to have fortified residences capable of standing up to sixteenth-century cannon, they would have built them.

Since not a few of the sixteenth- and seventeenth-century aristocrats did continue to live in castles as the undeniable symbols of ancient nobility and of the honorable traditions of a military aristocracy – hence, for example, the extensive and regrettable works of Robert, earl of Leicester, at Kenilworth, or the many and better works of restoration by the redoubtable Lady Anne Clifford on her castles in the north – we must say again that in the last analysis the decline of the castle means the decline especially of its military and political importance. In consequence it is customary to seek evidence in the later Middle Ages for a lowering of the guard, a lesser degree of strength, a disproportionate emphasis upon domestic comfort and ostentation to the detriment of defence, an upsetting, in short, of the balance of residence and fortress which is the essence of the castle. In history, at least, what is sought is often found, and certainly

examples of this matter are not hard to find. Something less than absolute strength has already been noted in the late fourteenth-century quadrangular castles of Bodiam and Bolton-in-Wensleydale (figs. 68-71), and others of their type, dating from the fourteenth and fifteenth centuries, are certainly no stronger while others verge upon the weak. A list, which does not claim to be complete, may include Maxstoke (*c.*1345), Shirburn (*c.*1380), Wingfield (Suffolk, *c.*1384, fig. 94), Caister-by-Yarmouth (*c.*1432), neighbouring Baconsthorpe (mid-fifteenth-century), Herstmonceux (*c.*1440, fig. 95), Oxburgh Hall (*c.*1480, fig. 96) and Hever (*c.*1482). Some at least of these before the end are shading off into the indeterminate class which we call fortified manors rather than castles. We are not far away, one feels, from the great Tudor house, moated perhaps for security (Playford Hall

95 *Herstmonceux in Sussex belongs to the 1440s (though much restored and altered) and to the category of fortified manor, comparatively lightly defended, as opposed to the castle proper. Water keeps malefactors at their distance and the main entrance is grandly machicolated.*

96 *Though substantially altered in the eighteenth and nineteenth centuries, Oxburgh Hall in Norfolk was not intended to have great strength even when built in c. 1480. It is and was a gentleman's country seat, providing security and evoking lordship by castellated architectural forms, not least the soaring but chiefly symbolic gatehouse.*

or Helmingham in Suffolk), or with a crenellated gatehouse for security and to evoke the past (Layer Marney; Hampton Court, fig. 97), but not at all seriously defended.

FORTIFIED MANORS

Yet it is a mistake to associate the lightly defended fortified manor house exclusively with the late Middle Ages, and thus associate it also with the decline of the castle, for the good reason that it had always existed from the time of the Norman Conquest, and the Conqueror's Domesday Book itself (1086) records 'defensible houses' (*domus defensabiles*). The castle, after all, was a fortified residence: it is the degree of fortification which distinguishes the castle from the house: that degree will often vary and the borderline between the two will always be, and always was, difficult to define. Defined it had to be at the time, because kings and other lords were concerned to control fortification. A castle without licence, thus, was 'adulterine' and liable to summary demolition. In Norman England the criteria were evidently settled as the depth of ditches, the height of banks, and the defensible strength of palisades. Later the single criterion came to be battlements, i.e. crenellation (which is as silly a piece of arbitrary bureaucracy as any modern instance) and hence those 'licences to crenellate' which abound in English royal records. But the law aside, not all the residences even of the great were castles, and if you wished to build a house of consequence you chose according to local circumstances, your needs and your resources, your status or pretension. The result, especially but not always for lesser men than nobles, might often be the fortified manor. We, in studying these matters, are limited by chance survival but, as it happens, two of the best-known fortified manors in England, at Stokesay (fig. 98) and Acton Burnell (fig. 99), date from the late thirteenth century, the very period, that is to say, of some of the greatest castles. The former is particularly interesting socially as the strong house (not really a castle though now given the courtesy title) of Laurence of Ludlow, reputedly the richest wool merchant

97　*Hampton Court is a great palace, begun by Cardinal Wolsey and completed (in its Tudor phase) by Henry VIII. It is not fortified and is not a castle but retains, like other Tudor buildings including Cambridge colleges, certain features of castellated architecture as in its Great Gatehouse and crenellations.*

98　*Stokesay in Shropshire is the type of fortified manor rather than castle proper. Though once surrounded by a high curtain wall, it otherwise consists of a hall and chamber block with a tower at either end. It was principally built between c. 1285 and 1305 by Laurence of Ludlow, a (very) rich wool merchant.*

99 *Elegant but barely defensible, Acton Burnell in Shropshire is an early example of a fortified manor, built in the 1280s by Robert Burnell, bishop of Bath and Wells and chancellor to Edward I.*

in the realm and a creditor of the king himself, evidently when it was first built (*c.*1285) setting himself up as a country gentleman when country gentlemen were knights. Acton Burnell, on the other hand, was built in the 1280s by no less a man than Robert Burnell, friend and counsellor to the same King Edward I, chancellor of England and bishop of Bath and Wells. Clearly he could have done better had he wished, i.e. built bigger and with a greater parade of military strength, but this small, elegant, sophisticated residence, with only a gesture of turrets and crenellation, seemed appropriate.

PELE TOWERS

This is the place also to mention, among fortified residences which are yet not castles, the so-called 'pele towers of the north', dating from the fourteenth and fifteenth centuries or later, and on both sides of the Border, which are the result of Edward I's failure to conquer Scotland, and the product of the endemic warfare, raids and counter-raids which followed between the English and the Scots. The word 'pele' has been made confusing by its transference (chiefly by nineteenth-century antiquarians) from its root meaning of a palisaded enclosure (hence 'paling' and 'beyond the pale') to the thing enclosed, i.e. the tower. The pele tower thus defined is simply a tower, usually rectangular, forming the fortified residence, the strong house, of the owner – a lesser tower keep, in short – standing within what is often called the 'barmkin' which is simply a small, walled courtyard, itself lacking the niceties of flanking towers and gatehouse and intended chiefly to protect animals and crops from marauders. The pele towers vary in size and elaboration from the almost insignificant proportions and extreme simplicity of the Vicar's Pele at Corbridge (fig. 100) to the more imposing structures at Chipchase (fig. 101) or Belsay, with their crenellated and machicolated parapets. The internal arrangements are commonly of two residential floors, each comprising one main room with or without lesser chambers, above a basement. At Sizergh there is a projecting rectangular turret (the Deincourt Tower) incorporated in the middle of the south side and rising some 10 ft above the battlements of the main tower. Others of the more elaborate towers, like Chipchase and Belsay, have one or more short projecting wings containing the staircase, entrance and small chambers. Elsewhere the stairs were commonly in an angle of the tower, and the entrance, like that of tower keeps and for the same reason, is often at first-floor level. But whatever the architectural details it is clear that these peles are, so to speak, the lesser castles of lesser men, and the fact should not be obscured by the use of a different terminology – they, like the even more enigmatic 'bastles' (cf. *bastille, bastide*), were raised all over the Border counties by gentry and less, men who had evidently not previously felt the need to fortify their houses. For them there was no question, economically or socially, of an elaborate and vastly expensive castle, nor was this necessary for the type of sporadic raiding and cattle-rustling in which they found themselves engaged, nor did they for the most part have any lordship to defend or to assert. It is, however, of particular interest to us that they often used, scaled down to their

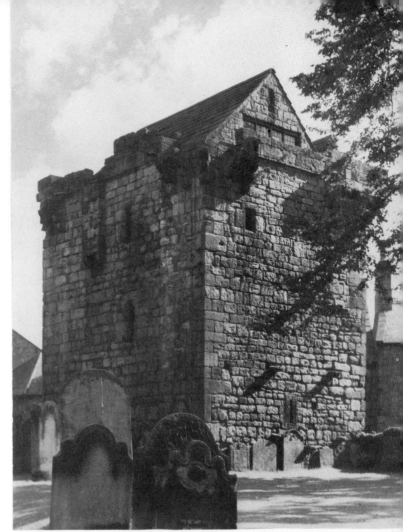

100   *The Vicar's Pele at Corbridge in Northumberland is a small and simple example of a 'pele tower', dated to c. 1300.*

101   *The pele tower at Chipchase, Northumberland, of mid-fourteenth-century date, with later windows and a later house (1621) attached to the east. The tower has a vaulted basement with three single-chamber residential floors, plus a machicolated parapet with bartizans at the angles.*

102 *Always one of the major castles in the realm and still the residence of England's premier duke (Norfolk) and Earl Marshal, Arundel in Sussex was much rebuilt in the late nineteenth century. It retains, however, amongst other ancient features, the original motte-and-bailey layout of the eleventh century, distinguished by two baileys and a fine twelfth-century shell keep upon the motte.*

own position and resources, the same fundamental type of fortified residence, i.e. the great tower, as had been used since the castle's beginning.

SURVIVAL

'And now it is all gone – like an unsubstantial pageant faded.' Thus James Anthony Froude on the passing of the Middle Ages. But in fact they are not gone, and medieval castles in particular are substantial buildings. Ruins abound, in every condition from undulations in the ground marking former earthworks to the towering structure of Caernarvon, which looks as though it could and should be finished and reoccupied tomorrow. Some even are still lived in by the fortunate few. In many cases continuous occupation was unbroken until the seventeenth century. Charles II restored and rebuilt the royal lodgings in the upper bailey at Windsor and lay at the Tower, as was traditional, the night before his coronation. The eighteenth-century attitude to castles was for the most part an ignorant pleasure in romantic ruins, but before that most philistine century was out the despised Middle Ages had their revenge in the beginnings of a Gothic Revival. The early Hanoverian monarchs scarcely visited Windsor castle, but in the 1780s George III began its restoration as one of the principal royal palaces of England, and was to spend £150,000 upon it between 1800 and 1814.

By 1840 his works and those of his two successors, George IV and William IV, under the direction of the architects Wyat and Wyatville, had made of Windsor what it is today (fig. 88) – 'to all intents and purposes a nineteenth-century creation, and . . . the image of what the early nineteenth century thought a castle should be' (*History of the King's Works,* vi, H.M.S.O., 1973, p. 392). It was in the late eighteenth and nineteenth centuries also that the great castles of Warwick (fig. 67), Alnwick and Arundel (fig. 102), for example, regained a former splendour at least as very stately homes, though too often Victorian 'restoration' came to be a less than sympathetic rebuilding (cf. their work on churches). Arundel castle as we see it now is almost nine-tenths the creation of the fifteenth duke of Norfolk, and thirty-sixth earl of Arundel and Surrey, between 1890 and 1903. A successful Victorian architect like Anthony Salvin might almost make a career from the restoration and rebuilding of castles (e.g. Alnwick, Windsor, the Tower of London) and he, indeed, even built a brand new castle for the first Lord Tollemache at Peckforton in Cheshire. There are, in fact, worse castles than Peckforton, and at times it may seem that the romantic and sentimental student of the medieval past cannot win. To come across a ruin, however beautiful or impressive, is to regret that it is ruined. Yet a castle which has been continually occupied will be no less damaged, whether that occupation is by families as at Arundel or Alnwick, or by some official agency of the Crown – the army, perhaps, at Dover, the Ordnance and the Armouries at the Tower, or Lancaster or Oxford castles serving out their time as prisons. Nowadays modern taste and modern techniques of restoration can or could do better had we not lost or taken away the resources for such expensive enterprise. Meanwhile owners, noble and common, do their best, and the castle still has also two good friends, though both are said to be hard-pressed: the National Trust and (still, at the time of writing) the Ancient Monuments branch of the Department of Environment.

6 The Castle in Peace and War

PEACE

That the castle from the beginning and throughout its history was at least as much a residence as a fortress has already been emphasized in this book, and the point is important both as a matter of historical truth and also in order that the buildings which survive may be understood. They may be still better understood if a little more is said, especially by way of illustration, about lordly life at the castle level – though it must also be pointed out again that not all the residences of the great were castles, or fortified manors, even in the feudal period. Most bishops did not occupy castles, though some did (the bishop of Winchester had several, including Farnham (fig. 16) which is still his; the Bishop of Durham had, amongst others, Durham (fig. 103), which is now a college of the university). But the king also had unfortified palaces, manor houses and hunting lodges, of which the most famous are Westminster Palace itself (now the site of the Houses of Parliament, though the Jewel Tower of the original building remains), Clarendon in Wiltshire, and Woodstock (now the site of Blenheim Palace after Queen Anne granted it to the Duke of Marlborough), and, though much less is known of them, other lords had their unfortified residences in addition to their castles, as the Black Prince had his palace at Kennington near the Oval.

One basic fact about medieval lordly life perhaps not generally realized is that everyone from the king downwards was itinerant, peripatetic, constantly on the move. It was this indeed that made possible the personal kingship and personal lordship of the age. As Marc Bloch observed (*Feudal Society*, p. 62):

Where transport is difficult, man goes to something he wants more easily than he makes it come to him. In particular, no institution or method could take the place of personal contact between human beings. It would have been impossible to govern the state from inside a palace: to control a country, there was no other means than to ride through it incessantly in all directions. The kings of the first feudal age positively killed themselves by travel.

Not too much should be made, indeed, of the difficulties of travel (which in any case did not change until the eighteenth century) for Top People in the Middle Ages were as much the Jet Set as now – the kings of England, for example, constantly crossing the sea to France, and bishops setting off for Rome at the drop of a hat. More than this, the magnates of the realm, clerk and lay, were of course expected to attend the King's Majesty at court, but were also ever on the move about their 'honors' and estates (usually widely scattered), from castle to castle and manor to manor, for they too had great matters to attend to and administration

103 *Aerial photograph of Durham (1948). The great Norman cathedral and the Norman castle (with its motte) stand side by side upon the rock, respectively symbolizing the 'Two Swords' of ecclesiastical and secular society, at Durham both in the hands of the bishop.*

104 *Saumur (Maine-et-Loire) from the fifteenth-century* Très Riches Heures du Duc de Berry. *The duke's castles illustrated in this famous manuscript are no less authentic for being shown as the very stately homes of a great noble of the age.*

may seem to us, of extreme formality, pomp and circumstance, with unavoidable informality and earthiness – the captains and the kings, the eagles and the trumpets, in the mud – which characterizes the medieval *dolce vita*, so that life at court in the twelfth century, for example, has been described by one historian as rather like a grand and perpetual picnic. In that life also, as it was led, castles were the staging posts and setting, and we should not be surprised to find, as we do, gardens, fishponds and dovecotes, parks and chaces, set in and about them.

Of all this the contemporary narrative sources, the chronicles and histories, and even the dry documents and records, often give us more than a glimpse across the centuries, and those castles soaring up prominently and proudly to the sky in the *Très Riches Heures du duc de Berri* (fig. 104), for example, are real, for they belonged to the duke. Gerald of Wales, twelfth-century churchman, courtier and man of letters, wrote of his family castle of Manorbier in Pembrokeshire in terms much like a more modern description of a gentleman's country seat – which, indeed, amongst other things, it was.

The castle called Maenor Pyrr . . . is distant about three miles from Penbrock. It is excellently well defended by turrets and bulwarks, and is situated on the summit of a hill extending on the western side towards the seaport, having on the northern and southern sides a fine fish-pond under its walls, as conspicuous for its grand appearance as for the depth of its waters, and a beautiful orchard on the same side, enclosed on one part by a vineyard, and on the other by a wood . . . . On the right hand of the promontory, between the castle and the church, near the site of a very large lake and a mill, a rivulet of never-failing water flows through a valley, rendered sandy by the violence of the winds. Towards the west, the Severn sea, bending its course to Ireland, enters a hollow bay at some distance from the castle.

A century later a more poignant, but equally domestic, note is struck by Joinville in his Memoirs of St Louis (i.e. Louis IX, King of France) concerning his departure on crusade, from which, of course, he might

to be done or seen to be done. As for the kings, they indeed wore themselves out with travel, ceaselessly peregrinating their realm, north, south, east and west. King John, for example, whose almost every move is known, seldom spent more than one or two nights in the same place, and he lived no differently from his more immediate predecessors and successors. Towards the end of the medieval period government became more sedentary and the pace of the itinerary slackens, but meanwhile it explains much. Since castles were residences, it partly helps to explain why there were so many of them, as it also explains why so many were more than half empty more than half the time, run by a skeleton staff. It also accounts for that basic domestic unit of medieval lordly life, the itinerant household, and it may in part account for the evident fitness of those who survived the rigours of their life, for they travelled in all weathers, and the men on horseback. That life must also help our understanding of that curious blend, as it never return, and could not for what was likely to be years. He received his scarf and pilgrim's staff from the Abbot of Cheminon, and immediately afterwards 'quitted the castle of Joinville without ever re-entering it until my return from beyond the sea.' Before his embarkation he tells us how he visited various local shrines in his own countryside and on one occasion in so doing passed within sight of his own castle. But, he writes, 'I dared never turn my eyes that way for fear of feeling too great a regret, and lest my courage should fail on leaving my two fine children and my castle of Joinville, which I loved in my heart.'

The building accounts and subsidiary documents, which in the splendid continuity of English history still survive at least from the royal administration, also give intimate glimpses of lordly life in castles. Henry II caused a garden to be made before his chamber window at Arundel (fig. 102). The same king's works at Windsor (fig. 88) included new royal lodgings on the north side of the upper bailey (where Edward III's state apartments now stand), set about a courtyard and a herb garden, and at Winchester he ordered work upon the castle chapel of St Judoc, the kitchen and a 'house' for the royal falcons, the painting of the king's chamber and the preparation of another chapel for the 'Young Queen', i.e. the wife of his son Henry, the 'Young King', who was crowned in his father's lifetime. King John commanded new kitchens to be built in his castles of Marlborough and Ludgershall, with ovens big enough to roast two or three oxen in each, and at his favourite castle of Corfe built for his own residence the beautiful and sophisticated 'Gloriette', again a courtyard house, now viciously 'slighted' with the rest of that castle by the victorious seventeenth-century Parliament after the Civil War. At royal Windsor Henry III in 1236 refurbished the queen's chamber in the upper bailey for his bride, Eleanor of Provence. Glass was set in two of the windows overlooking the garden, with shutters to open and shut, and another glass window, in the gable, was painted with the Tree of Jesse. In 1239 a nursery was built for their first-born son, the future Edward I, and later, one of Eleanor's chambers was to be painted 'of a green colour with gold stars', while the suite of Edward III's queen, Philippa, also at Windsor, included a chamber hung with mirrors and 'la daunsyng Chambre'. Everywhere within the apartments of castles there was colour, on windows, wainscot, plaster and rich hangings, and some castles were rendered with whitewash outside also, hence White Castle (Llantilio) in Monmouthshire and the White Tower at London. We have much less written information about baronial castles in this respect as in all others, but we may be sure that life within them was lived in the same fashion and almost to the same standard, and we may end this section with a description of Raglan by a fifteenth-century Welsh poet, with its 'hundred rooms full of festive fare, its hundred towers, parlours and doors, its hundred heaped-up fires of long-dried fuel, its hundred chimneys for men of high degree'.

The residential role of castles combined with the fact that they were undoubtedly strong places also explains many of their ancillary and often non-military uses. As the seats of kings and magnates, and more permanently of their officials, they were often the centres of local government and administration. Thus royal castles frequently housed the sheriff's office, and baronial castles the office of the lord's steward. It was therefore in the castle, in the hall, that the local court might be held (as until recently it was at Oakham (fig. 65), and at Winchester still is), and to the castle that a man might repair to plead his suit, present his services, pay his taxes or his rent. Watched by the porter, there passed through its gates a stream of people busy with their daily affairs, and to this day there are some castles which have remained the offices of local government, thereby to be preserved or mutilated. By virtue of its strength, also, the castle might have other specific uses, as treasury, perhaps, or armoury or prison. King John, in particular, laid his treasure up in certain of his castles, that it might be more immediately available as he moved about his realm, and a royal mint (eventually, and until the nineteenth century, *the* Royal Mint – hence Mint Street in the western outer bailey) was early established in the Tower of

105 *A late-fifteenth-century manuscript showing Charles, duke of Orleans (taken at Agincourt) imprisoned in the White Tower at London. Castles were used for the incarceration of high-ranking prisoners because they could provide appropriate accommodation as well as security. This illustration may help to dispel lingering popular notions of dank and dismal dungeons.*

London. The Tower still houses, too, the Queen's Armoury, and some of the royal armourers have been there at least since the time of Edward I (in whose reign the king's carpenters at the Tower made a model timber castle for his son, Alphonse – no toy, we may suppose, but meant to teach the military arts of siege-craft and defence). As for the castle's frequent subsidiary use as a prison, nothing has contributed more, although unjustly, to its popular notoriety – and has even changed the meaning in the English language of the honourable *donjon* to the deep, dark, dank, and entirely mythic

dungeon. Medieval records are indeed full of references to the castle gaol, and Henry II at the Assize of Clarendon in 1166 ordered that every county without a gaol should make one either in a castle or a borough. But the prisoners in castles included not only local offenders and common criminals awaiting trial (imprisonment was not used as a legal punishment) but also high-placed political prisoners of war and state (fig. 105), for the castle was not only obviously secure but also contained accommodation suitable to their rank (i.e. not 'dungeons' and oubliettes). The fate of such persons could be tragic. Thus Eleanor, 'the Beauty of Brittany', sister of Arthur of Brittany whom John is suspected of murdering for his claim to the English throne, was incarcerated for forty years (until her death in 1241) in the castles of Bristol and Gloucester, albeit honourably, with her

106 *A fifteenth-century siege of a castle (drawbridge firmly closed) by land and sea, showing longbows, crossbows, hand-guns and various devices (B.L. Royal 14 E IV).*

ladies in waiting and her robes supplied by the king. Nevertheless such unhappinesses are vastly overdone by guides and guidebooks, and never more than at the Tower of London which the innocent visitor might well suppose to have been purpose-built by Henry VIII for the imprisonment, torture and eventual beheading of his political opponents, real and alleged. Yet in fact that noble royal castle was only used on a large scale as a political prison for about a century after the monarch ceased to reside there and it therefore lost its primary function. If those bogus ravens were shooed away or shot, the medieval history of the Tower and England would be better served.

WAR

Nevertheless the castle was at all times before the sixteenth century also a fortress, and, although it has been emphasized above that its military role was at least as much offensive as defensive, it was built to be defended and defence accounts for 90 per cent of its design at any period (fig. 106). That defence, of course, was developed to counter the means of assault open to the assailants – though we must also note that attack is often thought to be the best means of defence, not least by the aggressive knighthood of the feudal period, and one remedy against siege and investment was the counter-attack or sally, often delivered through unexpected subsidiary gates, the sally-ports and posterns.

The means of attack in the Middle Ages, as in any age, can be divided roughly into close assault and bombardment. Long before the invention of gunpowder the period had its artillery, in the form of siege 'engines', usually stone throwing, which in fact long remained more effective than guns. Their range was not great but out of bowshot, and they were used, of course, to make a breach and soften up the target. There were two, perhaps three, main types. The *mangon* or *mangonel* worked on the principle of torsion. A long arm, with a cup or sling for the projectile at its free end, passed through a skein of ropes stretched between upright posts. The ropes were twisted towards the target and the arm pulled down against the torsion and, being released, hurled the projectile against the castle. The *trebuchet* (fig. 107), brought into common use, it is thought, in the later twelfth century, was capable of greater power and accuracy. Here again the projectile was hurled against the selected point in wall or tower by the free end of a long arm pivoted between two upright posts, but the motive power was provided by a counter-weight at the other and shorter end. It was less affected than the mangonel by weather (i.e. damp or dryness of the ropes of the latter) and power and range could be regulated by adjusting the mass of the counter-weight and its position on the arm. Both mangonel and trebuchet normally threw specially prepared stone balls or projectiles, though they might be used with the dreaded 'Greek fire', a combustible material modernistic in its effect, and a fourteenth-century illustration of a trebuchet loaded with a dead horse suggests an approach to germ warfare. The third type of engine, the *ballista* or *springald* more usually shot iron shafts or bolts or heavy javelins, and was thus, with its flatter trajectory, best suited to picking off defenders on walls and battlements. It worked on the principle of tension, i.e. the principle of the bow, and was in practice like an enormous crossbow – though to say that is to reverse development, for the hand-crossbow was developed from the Roman ballista. As for guns fired by gunpowder to hurl their projectiles (again at first stone balls), they were certainly introduced into English warfare in the early fourteenth century by Edward III against the Scots, and may have been used by Edward I, also against the Scots, at the siege of Stirling castle in 1297. For long they were small and not very effective save, probably, to scare the horses, and when large ordnance and siege pieces, capable of firing balls like the older engines, were developed in the fifteenth century they were difficult to transport, while mangonel and trebuchet could be raised pre-fabricated upon the spot. However, the formidable Mons Meg still at Edinburgh castle was made about 1450 (but restored in 1829 having blown up in 1680), and with two such guns, called 'Newcastle' and 'London', the Earl of Warwick in 1464 was able to take Bamburgh castle, formerly thought impregnable.

In addition to the engines and the later guns, there were other devices for breaching castle and town walls, although at zero range. Crude but effective and of great antiquity was the battering ram, usually a large tree-trunk, scarped and capped with iron, and swung again and again on ropes from strong supports against masonry or (especially) gates until successful. Slightly more subtle was the bore, smaller and with an iron point, used preferably on sharp angles to work away the stones. Men with picks and crowbars could be used to the same effect, and though this was dangerous movable screens and penthouses could be used to protect both these assailants and those manhandling the

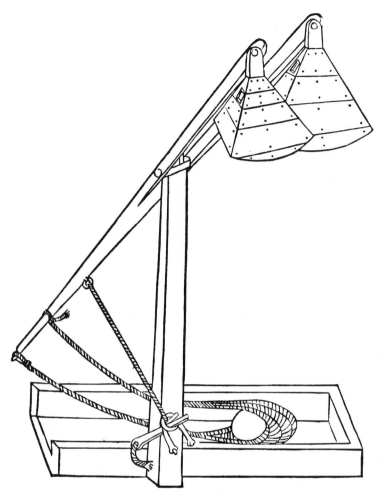

bore and ram. Far and away the most effective technique for the breaching of wall or tower, however, was undermining, nor, apart from the risky expedient of the counter-mine, was there any defence against it save to build one's castle on the living rock or set it in wide waters. The mine, of course, did not have to wait for the advent of gunpowder to fire it, and its earliest recorded use in England is by William the Conqueror at the siege of Exeter in 1068. The mining tunnel, begun at a distance and preferably out of sight, led to the mine gallery, set beneath that part of the defences to be brought down and shored up by pit-props. The chamber was then filled with brushwood and/or other combustible material. When all was ready, this was fired and the miners withdrew. If the job was done properly, the pit-props burnt, the masonry

107 *Medieval artillery. The trebuchet, seen here loaded with a shaped stone projectile, was worked by counterweights.*

above collapsed into the cavity of the gallery – and the besiegers poured into the breach thus made. The most dramatic evidence surviving in England of the effectiveness of undermining is the keep at Rochester where one can still see, in spite of later reparations, where one whole section of the great tower was brought down by King John's miners in November 1215 (figs 28-30).

In the end, if a castle were not surrendered it had to be entered and taken; and if a breach could not be made by mine or engine, or time did not allow such a lengthy process, then the job had to be done by hand, i.e. by escalade. A sophisticated variant of the scaling-ladders then required was the 'belfry' or great moveable tower, put together on the spot like the siege-engines themselves. Pushed up against the castle walls (a section of ditch or moat must first be filled in for the purpose) it enabled an attack to be launched upon the wall-head with a much greater concentration of force than the one-at-a-time method of the ladder. The belfry might also be used as a look-out post, and as an elevated shooting platform, perhaps commanding even the interior of the beleaguered castle. Thus at the siege of Bedford in 1224, Henry III commanded a wooden tower to be built and manned by archers and crossbowmen, to such effect that, according to the contemporary chronicler Roger of Wendover, no defender could ever remove his armour without fear of a mortal wound.

The assailants lacked, for themselves and their devices, the protection which the castle so lavishly provided for its defenders. Hence the movable penthouses, again constructed on the spot, under cover of which they could move up to the base of the walls and towers to work upon them, and the large shields or screens set up to give cover to archers and crossbowmen. Such penthouses, and also the belfries and siege engines, might also be covered by raw hides, or even metal plates, as a defence against being set on fire. Finally, we should note that all these devices were often given fanciful names which may make the reading of contemporary accounts of sieges startlingly confusing. Thus the penthouse shielding ram or bore may be the 'tortoise' or 'cat' from its slow or stealthy approach. The bore itself, picking or gnawing holes in masonry, may be called a 'mouse', and a belfry at the siege of Kenilworth in 1266 was known as the 'bear'. A favoured particular nickname for a stone-throwing engine was *Malvoisin* or 'Bad Neighbour', and so Prince Louis of France named his great *petraria* which he had sent over from France for his siege of Dover in 1216.

Against all this the defenders had first and foremost the strength and defences of their castle, developed, so to speak, externally precisely to resist all those known forms of attack. The need to keep an enemy at his distance is obvious, by broad water-defences or at least by dry ditch or wet moat. The double defence and outer screen of concentric fortification (e.g. fig. 87) fits the same context, and so does the barbican as an outer defence of the gate (figs. 61-2). To build your castle on the living rock is the best possible defence against undermining (e.g. figs. 80 and 82). When the fighting came to be at close-quarters, as medieval warfare usually was, the advantage of the projecting mural tower to lay down flanking fire from behind cover is paramount (fig. 48), and everywhere, indeed, we may see the castle's defensive superiority, in crenellation to give cover as well as apertures for shooting along the tops of towers and walls, in projecting timber hoarding (fig. 49) or stone machicolation (fig. 50), and in narrow arrow slits or loops unlikely to be penetrated by sharp shooters from without. The importance of all those immensely thick walls goes without saying, and we add their plinths or splayed-out bases, and sometimes the *glacis* or stone-paved bank on which the walls may stand. But in addition the castle's defenders had their own engines and devices as well as their personal weapons and strong right arms. The great stone-throwing engines were used in defence as well as attack, to destroy those of the attackers, and so was the springald. Guns, too, from their advent in the fourteenth century, were employed at least as much from within the castle as from without against it, as the gunports in later medieval fortification make abundantly clear. The desperate counter-measure of the counter-mine was used by the brave when necessary, and in other ways also defence might be offensive by the delivery of sallies and assaults via sally-ports and posterns. Nevertheless, though it can be argued, and in my opinion should be, that throughout the medieval period the techniques of fortification were superior to the means of attack upon it, no castle could hold out without supplies. The continuous series of records of royal expenditure, which in England survive from about the mid-twelfth century to the end of the Middle Ages (and of course beyond), make it abundantly clear that the preparation of castles for war involved supplies no less than men, at a cost which was no less, either. If those supplies ran out before the enemy himself was forced to withdraw, then the castle, however strong and strongly sited, must fall soon after.

Siege of Rochester

The best way to bring together and into focus the defence of and attack upon castles must be to choose and relate some of the more important sieges in English medieval history for which we have sufficient contemporary evidence. By doing so we shall also illustrate the superiority of defence in this period, for it is to be remembered that garrisons were usually numerically quite small and invariably much smaller than the besieging force, which had to be large completely to invest a fortress (and hence another military value of the castle, its ability, with an economy of manpower, either to control the surrounding countryside or to tie down large numbers of the enemy). Thus Rochester castle, commanding the crossing of the Medway and the main road of Watling Street from Dover and Canterbury to London, held out for almost two months, from 11 October to 30 November 1215, against King John and the army he was able to bring against it. It should be added that John, in spite of his popular reputation as 'Softsword', was no mean soldier, and very experienced indeed in fortification and siege craft. The taking of Rochester was one of the king's outstanding military successes, and it had a considerable effect upon his enemies in the civil war which closed his reign – as it was meant to do. 'After it', wrote the knowledgeable Barnwell chronicler, 'few cared to put their trust in castles.' The same writer also observed that 'Our age has not known a siege so hard pressed nor so strongly resisted.'

When the king arrived before the castle of Rochester, stone-throwing engines were at once set up to pound the walls. There were five of them according to the Barnwell chronicler, and Roger of Wendover, another contemporary historian, writes of a ceaseless barrage by day and night both from them and from the small-arms of bows and crossbows, one contingent of the royal forces relieving another. According to the former source the engines battered a breach in the wall of the bailey, but Wendover states that they achieved little and King John was obliged to employ the mine to gain entry. Evidently he is right, for there is a writ dated as early as 14 October, addressed to the reeves of Canterbury, commanding the urgent manufacture 'by day and night of as many picks as you are able', to be sent with all speed to the king at Rochester. In any event, when the bailey was breached and entered, the defenders in text-book fashion withdrew into the strongpoint and ultimate refuge of the keep. This certainly proved impervious to the battering of siege-engines and again John called upon his miners, this time to undertake the daunting task of breaching the massively constructed great tower (figs. 28-30). This they duly did. The mine was set beneath the south-east angle, presumably close to the breach in the bailey wall. Another writ, dated at Rochester on 25 November, commands Hubert de Burgh, John's justiciar and deputy-head of his royal government, to 'send to us with all speed by day and night forty of the fattest pigs of the sort least good for eating, to bring fire beneath the tower.' The bacon fat was needed to fire the pit-props shoring up the undermined foundations of the doomed keep, and in due course the whole south-east section of the tower came down – as may clearly be seen today in the obvious rebuilding carried out a few years later and visible both inside and out. At the time, however, not even this classic demonstration of the shattering effect of the mine brought about the immediate capitulation of the castle, though the end was near. With one side of the keep breached and half-collapsed, the defenders withdrew behind the cross-wall which divided the great building (page 38) and continued their resistance in the other side. 'Such was the structure of the stronghold', wrote the Barnwell chronicler, 'that a very strong wall separated the half that had fallen from the other.' Matters, however, could not long continue so. The desperate state of the defenders was made worse by a growing shortage of provisions. They were reduced to a diet of horse-flesh and water, 'which bore hardly on those who had been brought up in luxury' (Barnwell again). First they expelled those of their number least capable by now of fighting, and soon afterwards all of them were taken by the victorious king. John at first wanted to hang all the nobles among them – which, by the laws of war he was entitled to do since the castle had not surrendered but been taken by storm – and was only dissuaded by one of his captains who urged that such action would lead to retaliation against royal castles and so weaken the will of their defenders to resist. In the event, only one captured rebel was hanged – a crossbowman whom the king had maintained in his household and retinue since boyhood – and the Chancery enrolments are swollen with long lists of names of prisoners from Rochester sent for incarceration at Corfe and other royal castles. The king and his armies rode on, to the north and into East Anglia, where castles surrendered to him almost at his nod.

Siege of Dover

The siege of Dover in 1216 was another action in the civil wars which ended John's reign. This time the castle – 'the key of England' in the dramatic phrase of Matthew Paris, the thirteenth-century chronicler – was held for the king and attacked by Prince Louis of France, the appointed leader of the rebel forces and a rival claimant to the throne. The great castle on which Henry II had spent so much, and John after him, held out, but only just, and again it was the skilful setting of a mine which brought down its formidable defences. Louis concentrated his efforts against the main outer gate which King John had built at the northern apex of the castle (figs. 51 and 77), and succeeded first in taking the barbican or outwork which defended it. Then he directed a mine against the gate itself, and brought down the eastern of its twin towers. The royal constable and commander, Hubert de Burgh, and his knights were able to plug the breach with timber baulks and their own right arms, and continued to hold the castle until the death of John occasioned the withdrawal of Louis and the end of the war. But a weakness in the castle had been demonstrated, and amongst the extensive post-war works and reparations at Dover John's northern gateway was closed and blocked for all time by conversion into the present formidable trinity of the Norfolk Towers, and a new main outer gateway built to the west instead, which is the splendid Constable's Gate still there today.

Siege of Bedford

The siege of Bedford castle in 1224 had the still more dramatic result of the total demolition of the castle which had dared to stand for eight weeks against the majesty of the new king, Henry III, with all the force he could command. Again, as at Rochester, we have a near-perfect example of a full-scale investment carried through to its completion, with this time an even greater abundance of contemporary written accounts supplemented by the ample evidence of official records to provide detailed information. The lord of the castle (who was not in it at the time), Fawkes de Bréauté, a former captain of King John, now increasingly out of favour and called upon to give up the castle, had further defied the king by the capture and imprisonment at Bedford of a royal judge. When the young king came against the castle, the operation was begun by the Church Militant in the person of the archbishop of Canterbury, no less, who personally excommunicated the defenders. Then the secular arm of the kingdom began the assault by the raising of siege engines. The chronicler of the nearby priory of Dunstable describes their number, type and disposition. One *petraria* (probably a trebuchet) and two mangonels were set up on the east, two mangonels on the west which plied against the keep, and one mangonel on each of the north and south sides of the castle. In addition, two strong and lofty belfries were raised to overlook the beleaguered fortress, and filled with crossbowmen. By day and night the besieged had no rest from the shower of bolts and the thunderous pounding of the great stones against their walls and towers. For their part, the defenders had no thought of surrender but, on the assumption that their lord Fawkes would relieve them, maintained a determined defence and inflicted considerable losses upon the royal forces. Another contemporary chronicler, Ralph of Coggeshall, tells us that a certain lord, Richard de Argentan, was severely wounded in the stomach by a crossbow bolt which pierced his armour, that six other knights of the king's army were killed, as well as over two hundred of the men-at-arms and labourers manning the engines. With the arduous necessity of a prolonged siege and the mounting losses, bitterness grew, and the king swore that the garrison should hang if the castle was taken by storm.

Although, as the direct result of these events, almost nothing of the castle now stands above ground save for the truncated remains of its former motte, we can still follow the various phases of the siege, which was conducted like a text-book operation. Bedford was taken, the Dunstable chronicler tells us, in four main assaults. First the assailants took the barbican or outwork, losing four or five men in the action. Next, with heavier losses, they stormed and took the outer bailey, and captured with it a great part of the defenders' equipment and provisions – horses and harness, hauberks and other armour, crossbows, livestock and corn. Then they were faced with the inner and final defences, evidently the inner bailey (a section of whose stone-revetted ditch has recently been discovered in the south-east quarter of the former castle adjacent to the motte) and the tower keep which stood upon the motte. For these the miners were brought in. First they breached 'the wall next the old tower', which is presumed to have been the inner bailey wall near the keep. The subsequent capture of the inner bailey was achieved only with great difficulty and further losses including ten of the king's men who, attempting to press the victory home too ardently, were captured by the defenders and carried off into the ultimate refuge of the great tower on the motte. In the final act of the drama the miners again played the crucial role. On the Vigil of the Assumption (14 August), towards Vespers, writes the Dunstable chronicler, the mine beneath the keep was fired. Smoke poured into the inner rooms where the defenders were gathered, the tower sank upon its foundations, great cracks appearing down its sides. Further resistance was impossible. The ladies present, who included Fawkes' wife, Margaret, and the prisoners, including the captured judge, were sent out, and the royal standard was run up in token of surrender. The next morning, some eight weeks after the siege had begun, the depleted garrison were brought before the king and, having first been absolved from their excommunication, they, or the chief men among them, were hanged.

The surviving records also show us much of the organization and administrative effort which underlay the drama of the siege of Bedford as the king's government mobilized the resources of his kingdom against the castle. Thus siege-engines were carted from Lincoln and from Northampton and across Oxfordshire, while others were made on the spot by the many carpenters assembled there. The constable of Windsor was ordered to provide horses for Master Thomas and his fellow carpenters, together with their gear, 'so that they shall be able to travel to us by day and night as swiftly as they can and not delay'. Master Henry the carpenter came from Lincoln, and the sheriff of London provided horses for two other master carpenters, Walter and Simon, also to ride to Bedford. Timber was sent from Northamptonshire, and the monks of Wardon complained of the losses sustained when the king's men cut down trees in their woods. Ropes and cables for the engines came from London, Cambridge and Southampton; hides to protect them from fire and to make their slings were sent from Northampton; and tallow to lubricate them came also from London. To quarry, fetch and shape the stone balls for the engines' bombardment a small army of labourers was required, and the sheriffs of Bedfordshire and Northamptonshire were ordered 'without delay to cause to come to us at Bedford . . . all the quarries and stone cutters of your jurisdiction, with levers, sledges, mallets, wedges and other necessary tools to work stones for mangonels and *petrarie*.' Miners were sent from Herefordshire and the Forest of Dean by the constable of St Briavel's. Amongst the crossbowmen we read specifically of those coming from London, while orders went out to supply by the thousand the bolts or quarells for their weapons. Fifteen thousand were ordered up from the royal castle of Corfe, and the bailiffs of Northampton were commanded 'as you love us and our honour, that you cause to be made both by day and by night, by all the smiths of the town who are skilled in the art', four thousand quarells, well barbed and well flighted, to be sent with all speed to Bedford.

From the same records, too, we catch glimpses of the king's young majesty at war, his tents and pavilions spread (having been sent up from London in good and strong carts), and we can imagine them providing a colourful backcloth to the action, emblazoned with the royal arms, perhaps, and pennants streaming in the breeze. His arms and his war gear also came from London, while his personal requirements during the long siege included large quantities of wine together with almonds, pepper, saffron, ginger and cinnamon. At length, when all was over, the army was dismissed, the great engines dismantled and dispersed in storage, some to Northampton and some to the Tower of London, and the king's arms and baggage were also returned to London in the charge of Nicholas of the Chamber. The shattered castle of Bedford was razed to the ground, and Fawkes de Bréauté, deserted even by his wife, went into exile, to die a few years later.

Siege of Kenilworth

Not the least remarkable feature of the siege of Bedford in 1224 is that the castle, before it fell, held out for some eight weeks against the concentrated military resources of the whole kingdom. It is even more remarkable that in 1266 the castle of Kenilworth successfully withstood a similar concentration for no less than six months, and in the end was never taken but surrendered upon terms. These two facts could scarcely demonstrate more clearly the strength of the contemporary castle and the supremacy of defence over attack which it established. The siege of Kenilworth itself has all the romantic appeal of a lost cause, for the castle was held against the same King Henry III by a gallant band of the surviving supporters of Earl Simon de Montfort, the former rebel and would-be reformer of the realm, defeated and slain at Evesham the year before. The action was begun in earnest by the king and his son, the Lord Edward (the future Edward I) in June 1266. Resistance was still unbroken when, in mid-December, the defenders dragged themselves out of the battered castle. The full story of this major siege in English history cannot be given here, but two salient features need to be noted. The first is that the failure even after six months to take Kenilworth by force shows above all the value of broad water defences in denying the use of the mine. The second is the manner of its eventual surrender. By October, though the hope of relief which had borne them up all through the summer was not entirely gone, the condition of the defenders was becoming desperate through lack of supplies, including food. They therefore sought and obtained a truce of forty days, at the end of which they would give in if no help came. It did not come, and on 14 December when the term was up they yielded, and came out with the honours of war. The contrast with Bedford is obvious and significant. To yield a castle in hopeless conditions after a stout resistance was honourable and accepted, but the laws of war as then practised gave no necessary quarter when a fortress was taken by storm; and so it was at Bedford in 1224, and so King John had first thought to hang the garrison of Rochester in 1215 .

How now to end a book on English castles is far from clear. One certainly would not wish to end on a defensive note alone, and thus it must again be insisted that defence is at best only half the military role of castles, and their military role at best only half their medieval function. That said, it is also true that castles in England as elsewhere do not die but simply fade away. Their military value – which is, of course, what distinguishes castles from mere lordly residences – is the first to go, and yet may still linger even to the present day (Dover, for example, was both garrisoned and defended in the last war, when there were machine-gun posts also at Pevensey). Their residential role is still performed in many cases and, one hopes, will long continue. If it does not, then a certain type and style of lordship will have finally vanished. Perhaps such a social note is the one to end on, for castles above all symbolize historic lordship as they were meant to do, and the type of lordship they represent, feudal in origin, in England goes straight back to that most memorable date, 1066. Now that the captains and the kings have almost departed, the tourist as he approaches may no longer doff his cap, but he may yet feel impressed as he is meant to do, and by looking about him he will find not just a fortress but a way of life – of life in the Middle Ages, at the top.

Index